REIKI'S

BIRTHPLACE

Published by:
Infinite Light Healing Studies Center, Inc.
P.O. Box 1930
Sedona, AZ 86339
www.InfiniteLight.com

Design/layout: Ian Shimkoviak/Alan Hebel (aliandesign.com)
Editing: Barbara Mayer, Laurelle Shanti Gaia, Mari Hall,
Lane Badger, Linda Crawford.

ISBN: 978-0-9678721-4-8

NOTE TO THE READER: Every attempt has been made to
ensure the information contained herein is valid at the time of
publication. The publisher however, reserves the right to make
changes, corrections and/or improvements at any time and
without notice. In addition, the publisher disclaims any and all
liability for damages incurred directly or indirectly as a result of
errors, omissions or discrepancies.

Printed in China through Alian Design.

REIKI'S
BIRTHPLACE

A GUIDE TO KURAMA MOUNTAIN

JESSICA A. MILLER

FOREWORDS BY
WILLIAM LEE RAND,
LAURELLE SHANTI GAIA
& WALTER LÜBECK

ACKNOWLEDGEMENTS

I AM PROFOUNDLY THANKFUL TO ALL of those who helped make this book a reality. Even more so than with most books, this book could not have happened without you. Thank you all those willing to read and translate Japanese for me, and for their patient explanations. Thank you to my translator and friend Ayumi. Thank you to Hyakuten for his knowledge and kindness; Linda Crawford, my friend and 'voice', for talking with the people of the mountain and her able editing assistance. For their insights, I wish to thank Tomoko of Kurama, and my friends Gabi Hadl and John Walker. Thank you to all who previewed and encouraged the manuscript, including Liz Mitchell, for editing an early version. Walter Lübeck who gave me encouragement when I really needed it. Laurelle Shanti Gaia and Michael Arthur Baird of Infinite Light Healing Studies Center in Sedona, AZ and Barbara Mayer, their editor and their artists for editing and publishing this. Thank you for the many people in Kurama village and Kurama temple who got to know me on sight and made me feel welcome, even if we could not speak the same language. Thank you to all those I met 'by chance' on the mountain who allowed me to share what I knew, and who were willing to translate signs and share what they knew with me. Ayumi Ikushima provided the majority of basic translation of the various signs and temple documents used in the process of writing this book. Ayumi is an experienced translator of both written and spoken Japanese, English and French. Her enthusiasm, willingness to explain her culture, and kindness, were key to making this book a reality. I appreciate Barbara Matsuura who was willing to take me and Dennis Hescox through Japan, and show us the ropes and Judith Clancy for her willingness to share her wisdom and experience of Japan, Reiki and book publishing.

Thank you to all my teachers of Reiki and other ener-getic ways of seeing the world, including Reiki teachers Liz Tarr and William Rand, Tom Cowan, Jonathan Goldman, and Jennifer Moore. Thank you for all who believed I could do this, especially my parents Joe and Kathy Bush, Ross Miller, Carl Landsness and Jeff Walters. Thank you to all my Reiki students for their love and support.

Thank you for all of the energies of Kurama and Kyoto and Reiki that conspired to make this book possible. Thank you to the spirit of Mikao Usui, and the Bodhisattvas Kwan Yin (Kannon) and Jizō.

TABLE OF CONTENTS

FOREWORD

H UMAN BEINGS HAVE SOUGHT PLACES OF POWER within nature since the beginning of time. Whether it be a cliff overlooking an ocean, a waterfall, desert, or mountain, people have found solace in the dramatic presence of nature. Such a place of power is created outwardly by a combination of forces that together form an ambience of unusual beauty and peace. Inwardly perceived, there is also an attracting focus of subtle energies, energies that refresh and renew and draw one up into spiritual realms. Some of these places remain in their natural state, wild, raw, and untouched while others are graced by temples, shrines, and holy cities that honor the energy, focus the power, and provide a sanctuary for meditation and worship. Kuramayama is such a place of power. Sloping between two peaks and covered with cedar trees, this gentle mountain refuge is home to many temples and shrines. A trail leads to the top of the mountain on the village side, passing several small waterfalls and each of the spiritual sites. At the top, other trails lead through the forest, allowing the spiritual seeker opportunity for solitude and communion with nature.

I recall, once, after spending all day on the mountain, slowly beginning the descent, alone. The sun was setting, and the day slowly changing to twilight. The cooling air felt refreshing on my skin after a day of hiking. Tinged with fall color, shimmering leaves rustled ever so gently in the light breeze. A peacefulness imbued everything, gently caressing my soul. I drifted into the spell of the mountain and within this moment became aware of the unmistakable inner light of higher consciousness that is so often present where spiritual devotees have dedicated themselves to a life of meditation in pursuit of enlightenment. Being the birthplace of Usui Reiki, for the first fifty years or more that Reiki was practiced in the West, the location of Kuramayama was somewhat of a mystery, more of a legend than an actual place one could visit. Only in recent years has its location become widely known within Reiki circles, and Reiki pilgrims have begun making the journey of homage to the place which gave rise to their healing art.

To my knowledge, this is the first book written by a Reiki teacher in honor of the birthplace of Reiki that provides such a thorough description of its history, legends, and cultural background. It is a wonderful preparatory guide for those wanting to journey to this sacred mountain and gives those unable to go a thorough understanding of the importance of this magical place. Certainly it will help ground the reality of Reiki in the location of its origin and assist those devoted to Reiki to more completely embrace the source of the healing energy that flows through them.

—William Lee Rand
JERUSALEM, MARCH 2006

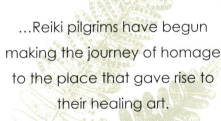

...Reiki pilgrims have begun
making the journey of homage
to the place that gave rise to
their healing art.

From my first serious trip to Japan in January 2001 to the fall of 2006, I have visited Kurama Mountain eighty times. In January 2001, I spent a week in Japan visiting the Usui memorial in Tokyo, the Meiji Mura Architectural museum in Nagoya, and just over a day in Kyoto before going back to Kurama Mountain. At the end of the day on Kurama, I felt called to come back. A single day on Kurama Mountain was just not enough. I came back in late September, and spent five weeks in Japan, most of it in Kyoto. During that time I took Reiki training with several Japanese Reiki schools, assisted as a guide to William Rand's group in Japan, and even taught a few Reiki classes. The most meaningful thing I did, however, was go up to Kurama Mountain twenty-one times during these five weeks as a personal pilgrimage and prayer for peace.

I arrived in Japan on Sept. 22, 2001, eleven days after the terrorist bombings of the Pentagon and World Trade Centers. As a Reiki practitioner, I set the intention to make twenty-one trips because Reiki's founder meditated on Kurama Mountain for twenty-one days, and at the end received Reiki. While I did not fast nor even spend the full day on the mountain during each trip, going twenty-one times gave me a goal and a spiritual focus, and on the day before I left, I went a twenty-second time, just because I missed going.

Many things happened in this time, some strong, some subtle, some I have yet to understand. By going day after day, I felt like I developed a relationship to this sacred place, a strong intuitive understanding and connection. My relationship to Kurama is similar to the relationship many coastal people have with the ocean. It is not enough to see it once and leave forever, but instead there is a need to continue to revisit it, in different weather and times of the day. Kyoto has many sacred, impressive, beautiful and fascinating places, but Kurama is the place that calls my heart. It is my delight to share it with you.

—Jessica Miller
AUTHOR - *Reiki's Birthplace*

Since visiting Kurama Mountain in 1997, I am eternally in love with the splendor and magnificence of this profoundly sacred ground. For Jessica's extensive research and the beautiful photos of Kurama Mountain that appear in this book, I am very grateful. As a publisher of *Reiki's Birthplace*, I speak for both Jessica and myself when I say it is our intention that everyone who encounters this book be blessed by the healing power of Reiki and the sacredness of Kurama Mountain. One of the fondest wishes of Usui Sensei was that Reiki be available for everyone. Usui acknowledged Reiki as a universal blessing for all the people of the world. As new paradigms and perspectives are transforming our world, I feel that Reiki is our pathway to the age of peace.

During my pilgrimage to Japan in search of the true history of Reiki, I would have loved a guidebook like this. Not only is this a great guide for those planning a visit to the mountain, it is an excellent educational resource for the dedicated Reiki practitioner and teacher. This book allows the reader to experience the essence of Kurama Mountain's serenity and power from anywhere in the world.

—Laurelle Shanti Gaia

Infinite Light Healing Studies Center, Sedona, AZ

Kurama Mountain is one of the most enchanting and magical places in the world. The wonderful tall trees with their mighty roots, the beautiful flowers, the springs and temples, the silent walkways and mystical shrines – this nourishes the soul and supports meditation, healing and the widening of consciousness. Each time I have been there was very special for me. They were moments which deepened my understanding of Reiki, of my own spiritual path, of life itself. Even if Dr. Usui, the founder of the Reiki healing system would not have had his *Satori* (enlightenment) here, it would be a very special place. I am happy that this book was written by someone very much dedicated to Kurama Mountain and its mysteries. Whenever I looked at the manuscript I felt the enchanting energies of Kurama. May this book help everyone interested in Kurama Mountain to understand and feel its delicate and very special spiritual energies.

—Walter Lübeck
GRANDMASTER OF RAINBOW REIKI

A MESSAGE FROM KURAMA TEMPLE:

Prior to publication, Kurama Temple officials were given a copy of the manuscript and requested excerpts concerning Mikao Usui and his relationship with the mountain. Below is their response.

"Kurama Mountain is open to all people. The energy of the mountain enables the people who feel a destiny to come to the mountain, to do so, and to find direction for their lives while receiving vitality and energy. Kurama Temple believes Mikao Usui was such a person."

WHAT IS REIKI?

Reiki is a form of holistic energy healing, which dramatically increases one's ability to transmit univeral life force energy, or"ki" (Chinese "chi"). The practitioner places their hands on or above the client, and if the client needs energy in a particular area, their body absorbs it. Reiki does not require the practitioner to hold any particular spiritual, religious beliefs or special skills,. However Reiki is similar to prayer in that it works for the highest good, regardless of the knowledge, wisdom or skill of the practitioner. Anyone can learn Reiki to help themselves, their family, and others.

SITE
GUIDE

INTRODUCTION

KURAMA MOUNTAIN (PRONOUNCED COO-RAH-MAH) is a sacred mountain due north of the Imperial Palace of Japan's former capital of Kyoto. In its twelve centuries of existence, as both a Buddhist and Shinto sacred place, the mountain has developed a rich tapestry of history and legend. Kurama is the name of the temple, the village and the mountain. This book focuses on the different sites on the Kurama Temple area (Kurama-dera in Japanese) from the perspective of a foreign visitor. Exploring Kurama Mountain is intended as a general guide for anyone interested in Kurama Temple. As a teacher of the energy-healing art called Reiki, which originated on this mountain, I have chosen to include information that is relevant for Reiki practitioners and others with an interest in spiritual energy.

Bright Blessings!
Jessica Miller
KYOTO, JAPAN

The copper roof of the Tenpōrin-dō Hall
which houses the Amida Buddha statue.

14

Kurama Mountain's main temple is two-thirds of the way up the mountain.

A children's picnic outside Kurama's museum.

17

Trains leave for Kurama from Demachiyanagi Station.

Train Ride To Kurama

Kurama Mountain is easily reached by train from Japan's ancient capital of Kyoto. Most visitors will get on the Eizan Densha line (or Eiden, for short) line at the ground level section of Demachiyanagi station, in northeast Kyoto. It is about a 25 minute train ride to the Kurama station. The tickets cost about 420 yen (around $4 US), each way. Tickets can be purchased on the train or at the end stations. The Kansai card (full name Surutto-Kansai Miyako Card) is also now accepted, and can be used on all of Kyoto's trains, subways and buses.

The train ride is very pleasant, passing by rice fields, small towns, Japanese graveyards and climbing up into the mountains. It is a nice way to get a sense of Japan, outside of the city. The seven-mile road from Kyoto to Kurama has existed since at least the late 700's. Summer visitors, peasants and emperors, would journey into the mountains to escape the summer heat. Priests and mystics would spend time in these mountains seeking supernatural healing powers, performing various meditations and spiritual practices. The train line from Kyoto to Kurama was completed in 1929, and ever since, the ride has been a favorite day trip for Kyoto visitors. This area of Kyoto is famous for its fall foliage. In November, thousands of visitors from all over Japan crowd the trains. Most get off at either Kibune or Kurama station to enjoy nature and visit the Kurama temple and Kibune shrine. During the prime foliage season, lights are placed in the trees along the tracks, creating an evening ambience of a fairy wonderland.

Ki Note

Scan your hand over the train station pictures to the left and notice the differences in their energy.

KI NOTE

ENERGY CHANGES: As the train climbs out of the suburbs and into the mountain forests, the natural 'ki' (life force) energy strengthens. The energy becomes more vibrant and alive, while assisting visitors in adjusting their energy field to a higher vibration. Some people can feel the energy better by facing backwards on the train.

REIKI HISTORY NOTE: The train did not exist until after Mikao Usui's death in 1926. Therefore, Mikao Usui must have hiked or taken some other form of transportation to get to the mountain.

Visitors get a beautiful view from inside the train.

KURAMA TRAIN STATION

Ⓘ N SHARP CONTRAST TO THE VERY MODERN Demachiyanagi
station, the Kurama train station is a pleasant wooden structure.
In the southeast corner of the station there is a table with a stamp
of Kurama station. Train enthusiasts, hikers and other visitors use
it to stamp their travel books as a souvenir (Bring your ink-pad
and paper, as the official ink-pad is often dry.) On the walls of the
station are some of the torches carried through the streets during
Kurama's famous Fire Festival which occurs annually on October
22. The men of the town carry the torches through the streets
along with portable shrines containing the deities of Kurama Temple's main Shinto site, the Yuki shrine.

Outside the station is a fifteen-foot wooden statue of the
head of Kurama's most famous legend, the Kurama Tengu. A
Tengu is a kind of Japanese goblin with red skin and a long
nose, famed for martial arts prowess and magic. During the
temple's busiest days, conductors dressed in Tengu costumes
will direct visitors through the station. A plaque commemorates the 1929 opening of the train line. While there is some
parking in the town for visitors, most come by train which
allows the town to preserve its quaint character.

A statue of the legendary Kurama Tengu outside the station.

PRACTICAL NOTE

Beyond the statue and parking lot, the road out of the train station quickly intersects with the main road through the village of Kurama. If planning to return to Kurama village, instead of hiking over Kurama Mountain to Kibune, pay attention to this intersection. The station is easy to miss if coming from the other direction. The Kurama station also has a ticket machine to buy the ticket for the return trip, and various vending machines where one can buy snacks and drinks. There are lockers on the outside of the station for storing purchases, coats etc. Using these lockers is fine if the visitor is only going as far as Kurama's main temple. However, if visitors are going over the mountain to the other side, they will not be returning to this train station. Visitors with some extra time in Kurama village may wish to go to Kurama Onsen. During most times of year, a free van meets visitors at the train station and takes them directly to the Onsen (If there is no van, look for signs directing visitors to the Onsen. It's about a 20-minute walk.) The Onsen is an outdoor public bath, with separate pools for men and women. For your first trip to a public bath, it is recommended that you bring with you someone who can speak Japanese. This way you can become acquainted with the rituals of where to put your shoes, and how to shower sitting on a stool. Most Japanese guide books will also discuss what to do.

Inside Kurama Mountain train station.

A view of the train station from Kurama Village.

Bring your own ink-pad to use with Kurama
Station's official stamp and a sheet of paper.

KURAMA VILLAGE

Walking into the village of Kurama is like walking into the past. Several of the stores have posted old photographs of the village (mostly from the 1920's), showing it to look much the same then as it does now. The village of Kurama grew due to the support of people going to Kurama Temple, when Kurama was still a favorite meditation and recreation spot for the nobility in Kyoto. The village was founded along with the temple around 770 A.D. Local shops sell Kurama souvenirs, pickled seaweed and Japanese sweets. There are also several Japanese restaurants. Continuing up the main street, the road curves to the

right and the Kurama temple is straight ahead. While there are many tourists who come to Kurama village and Kurama Temple, nearly all of them are Japanese. None of the shopkeepers speak English, but it is still relatively easy to buy souvenirs and sweets, without speaking Japanese. The employees in the village eateries do not speak English either, though one can easily communicate by pointing at what their neighbor is eating. Most restaurants have menus posted outside, which give an idea of the prices, even if one can't read the entries. One very special restaurant for the adventurous is on the right, partway up the stairs, just before the temple entrance gate. It serves very unusual vegetarian food, and does have an English translation of the menu. I splurged on the deluxe lunch that was about $30 a person. It had seaweed prepared four different ways, vegetarian sushi, various soups and other dishes. It was a very memorable meal.

Kurama's shops sell souvenirs to tourists.

Visitors wishing to explore the village beyond the entrance
to Kurama Temple will see the Kurama river, and an aqueduct
that brings water out of the river, past many of the homes. The
aqueduct allowed the homes along its banks to have running
water in times before the area added more contemporary in-
door plumbing. There are several stone masons in Kurama village who make stone lanterns and other outside decorations.
Kurama granite is famous.

Some of the buildings on Kurama's street
date back to the Middle Edo period in the 1700's.

Pickled daikon radishes, leaves and eggplant
are among many of the market's offerings.

REIKI NOTE

REIKI IS UNKNOWN ON KURAMA: Most Reiki practitioners are shocked to discover that Mikao Usui and Reiki are virtually unknown in Kurama. There are no Reiki shops, photos nor souvenirs. Reiki may have begun when Mikao Usui meditated here in the early 1900's, but except for the steady stream of foreign visitors who ask about it, it has left no trace.

DID USUI EAT HERE? Kurama village is remarkable because it has kept its appearance similar to when Usui was here. In Mrs. Takata's version of the Reiki story, after his Reiki experience, Mikao Usui stopped at an inn, ordered a big breakfast, and healed the innkeeper's granddaughter. Kurama village, or Kibune village on the other side of the mountain, are the most likely spots where this might have occurred.

Entrance to
Kurama Mountain Temple

Close-up of the temple's crest and shoes left by pilgrims.

FROM THE ROAD, CLIMB THE STAIRWAY up to the entrance of the Kurama temple. To the left of the stairway is an access road that was built during the 1930's. Construction on this road required that the temple's original entry gate be dismantled and moved over a few feet. There is an orange mailbox on a post to the left of the access road. Here visitors can mail postcards and receive a Kurama postmark. (Visitors must have their own stamps, however, as there is no place to purchase them.) The large building to the left of the entrance is actually a series of classrooms used by the temple. Kurama's entry is a 40-foot-tall wooden structure. The doors are always open, revealing the way up the mountain. Visitors enter the temple grounds (the whole mountain) by walking through this entryway.

The main entrance to Kurama Temple.

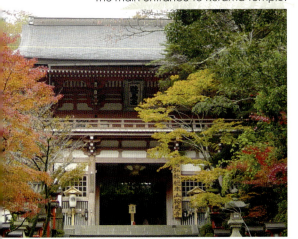

Looking down to Kurama village from the temple entrance. The main entrance to Kurama Temple.

The Entrance
and a Kannon Shrine

A S VISITORS FIRST ENTER THE TEMPLE, many will notice the paper lanterns with Kurama's crest. Many think the crest of the Kurama temple looks like a scallop sea shell, however, it is generally believed to be a stylized Tengu fan. Some will also say it is the imperial flower, the Chrysanthemum, as seen from the side. Notice the straw shoes that are attached to the area near the lantern. In earlier times people commonly wore this type of footwear. The pilgrim would wear the shoes until the objective of the journey was achieved, and would then leave them at the place where the journey was completed, signifying they need not travel in those shoes any longer. Modern visitors, indicating the completion of significant pilgrimages, left these shoes. Inside the wire grating, the Nio (the statue guardians) guard the temple's entryway. They are partially hidden in the alcoves of the temple gate. The Niō's purpose is to scare away 'evil spirits', and their stances reflect both active and passive power. Visitors step over the threshold of the open gate, and pay the 200 yen (a little less than $2 US) entry fee. The temple is 'officially' open from 9a.m. - 5p.m. most times of the year. The gates are never closed. Visitors receive a brochure about the temple in Japanese or English. Inside the gateway is a purification shrine dedicated to Kannon (Kwan Yin), one of the major deities of Kurama. To purify yourself, rinse both hands with water from the ladle. Then pour some water into your hand and rinse out your mouth.

Standing on either side of the temple's entrance in the alcoves, *Niō Guardians* protect the temple from evil spirits.

Visitors pay the entrance fee at the entry booth to Kurama.

This statue of Kannon (Kwan Yin) stands inside the temple entrance. Visitors use water from Kannon's statue to purify themselves.

Covers of the Kurama Mountain brochures in both English and Japanese.

NURSERY SCHOOL AND THE SIX JIZŌ

A SCENDING THE PATH, the next building on the right is the Kurama Temple Nursery School. Buddhist-run nursery and grade schools for local children have been common throughout Japan for centuries. They were originally responsible for Japan's high literacy rate, even before the government took over most education in the 1870's. In front of the school is a statue of six Buddha-like children called The Six Jizō. Real cloth bibs are placed on each child. The bibs are changed periodically by the people of the temple. On the accompanying sign is a Japanese poem: "All children are the children of Buddha. Children are heavenly gifts. Children are the mirrors which reflect the hearts of the parents."

Jizō (Sanskrit name Kshitigarbha) is one of the most beloved spiritual beings in Japan. He is considered the guardian of children, pregnant women, travelers and firemen. There are six Jizō depicted here, because Jizō has the keys to the Buddhist Six Realms of Existence. Originally he is the rescuer of souls lost in hell, including the souls of unborn children. Jizō's role as guardian of firemen relates to their job of going into the flames. He is the guardian of travelers because he traverses The Six Realms of Existence. His connection to children has always been a part of his friendly image. Jizō is typically seen carrying a pilgrim staff with rings that jingle when he moves, and he has a gem upon his forehead. There are typically six rings on the staff, signifying the Six Realms. Jizō is well represented on Kurama. In addition to The Six Jizō, there are three other temples on the mountain dedicated to him. One is near the Yuki Shrine, the other is near the top of the mountain. The third is near Nishimon Gate.

The Six Jizō: Jizō travels through the Buddhist Six Realms
of Reality to rescue lost souls, especially children.

PRACTICAL NOTE

The ladies restroom, across the fire road from the nursery, has a western-style, sit-down toilet . Everywhere else on the mountain, the public toilets are the Asian "squatter-style".

Crest on the Nursery School.

THE MAIN INFORMATION OFFICE

THE LARGE CONCRETE BUILDING ON THE RIGHT, after the nursery, is the Information Office and Cable Car station. This building acts as an auxiliary information office for those who do not wish to hike to the main temple complex. Outside, on the corners of the building are odd flower shaped chains called "rain chains" (kusari doi). They allow the rain falling on the roof to gracefully reach the ground. This Japanese style of rain gutter has been used for centuries. In days before running water, rain barrels would be placed under such rain chains to collect the water for household use.

Inside the building are several areas of interest. Opposite the door, there is an altar dedicated to the deities of Kurama Temple. (This altar is discussed in detail later in this chapter.) On the wall, to the left of the door, is a map of the mountain. It shows all of its temples and shrines. Kurama Mountain is a typical Japanese Buddhist mountain temple. There are temple sites all the way up and down the mountain. The map shows all of the mountain's sites (labeled in Japanese) and the location of the Kibune and Kurama train stations. A closed stairway leads to a second floor used for some temple functions. The one-person kiosk in the center of the room is the place to buy the 100-yen tickets ($1 US) for the cable car, and to ask questions (in Japanese) about the mountain. The person there also keeps an eye on the temple altar.

To the right of the altar is another room with benches. This is where visitors wait to board the cable car. (The cable car is described later in this chapter as well.) The building contains a number of framed Japanese documents including monthly inspirational messages. One such message reads: "Whatever the reason you come to this mountain, something can be given. So

Rain chain gutters.

feel the energy, power of heaven, and take a deep breath." You may also find information about the mountain's twelve native varieties of Tengu mushrooms, or a congratulatory statement for the safety record of the cable car. There are also several display cases which highlight different aspects of the mountain's history and festivals.

A map of Kurama's temples.

Information Office
and Sanmon Station.

THE ALTAR AT THE INFORMATION OFFICE

T HE ALTAR TO THE DEITIES OF KURAMA MOUNTAIN dominates the main room of the Information Office. This is the easiest altar on the mountain to examine.

THE DEITIES OF THE MOUNTAIN

This altar represents the three major deities of Kurama Mountain. From left to right, they are Maõ-son: The Power of Earth; Bishamonten: The Light of the Sun; and Kannon (Kwan Yin): The Love of the Moon. The philosophy of Kurama Mountain considers that, when these deities are linked together, they form an overarching universal deity, called Sonten. The central statue is of Bishamonten. The disks on the wall behind the altar are Sanskrit symbols representing the deities. On the altar table are offerings to these deities. Bishamonten is the deity for whom Kurama was founded. In the year 770, the temple's founder had a vision of being attacked by demons and being rescued by Bishamonten. In the Buddhist sacred book, *The Lotus Sutra*, Bishamonten is the deity who guards the north of the Buddha. He is considered a protector of those doing sacred things and one who brings wisdom and wealth. The people of Kurama Temple connect him to the light of the sun. Maõ-son is unique to Kurama Mountain. Temple writings say that this deity arrived from the planet Venus in a fiery vehicle five million-years-ago. The Kurama Tengu, Kurama's most famous legend, is considered to represent Maõ-son. Maõ-son's goal is to protect and encourage the spiritual evolution of mankind. Kurama temple associates him with the power of the earth. Kannon is more commonly known as Kwan Yin in English. Kannon is

Disks are painted with the Sanskrit symbols representing Kurama's deities. From left to right - Maõ-son, Bishamonten and Kannon.

known as the Goddess of Mercy. She is the one who hears the cries of those that call her name and will do her best to help. An early pilgrim to Kurama Temple saw visions of Kannon on Kurama, and built temples to her there. The people of Kurama Temple associate Kannon with the love of the moon, and consider her one of the three aspects of the deity Sonten.

A shrine to the deities of Kurama Mountain.
The center statue is of Bishamonten.

Reiki Note

ORIGIN OF SYMBOLS (LEFT): In addition to the basic healing energy, Reiki uses three focusing symbols, united under a single master symbol. While the connection cannot be proven, it is a circumstantially compelling thought that Kurama Mountain has a similar belief structure of three deities under a single master deity. Could Usui have been inspired by the idea of three energies under an overarching energy to conceptualize the energies of Reiki in a similar structure? In the absence of actual documentation from Mikao Usui, it can only be speculation, especially as there are other examples in Japan of deities with three aspects.

The Sanskrit symbol "Hrih" that here represents Kannon/ Kwan-Yin, is the likely origin of Reiki's mental/emotional harmony symbol.

INFORMATION OFFICE: PRAYER

O N EITHER SIDE OF THE ALTAR is inscribed the temple's Prayer to Sonten. The prayer gives a marvelous introduction to the philosophy of Kurama Temple. The following text is from the English language insert to the Kurama Temple brochure.

The Sonten of Kuramayama
The Spirit of the Moon … Love
The Spirit of the Sun … Light
The Spirit of the Earth… Power} The Triune Deity

Oh, Sonten, Beautiful as the Moon,
Warm as the Sun, Powerful as the Earth.

Bestow your blessing upon us to uplift mankind and increase our riches and glory.

In this holy place, grant that peace may defeat discord, unselfishness may conquer greed, sincere words may overcome deceit, and that respect may surmount insults.

Fill our hearts with joy, uplift our spirits, and fill our bodies with glory.

REIKI NOTE

REIKI-LIKE PRAYER: The religion of the followers of Kurama Temple has nothing to do with Reiki, yet it arose on the same mountain. It can be considered a sister-like energy to Reiki. A number of phrases in the prayer sound like Reiki prayers: "Fill our hearts with joy, uplift our spirits, and fill our bodies with glory." In the Japanese version of this prayer, the word 'lord' in "Great Lord of the Universe" is actually the character for "Rei", the same character we use for Reiki. Also, the title for Sonten as Great Light, is actually the Japanese Kanji "Dai Ko Myo", which is familiar to most Reiki Masters.

Sonten, Great Lord of the Universe, Great Light, Great Mover, bestow upon us who gather to worship you, upon those who strive to touch your heart, a new strength and a glorious light.

鞍馬山尊天幸福への祈り

鞍馬山尊天
月輪の精霊―愛―千手観音
日輪の精霊―光―毘沙門天
地輪の精霊―力―護法魔王尊
} 三身一体尊天

尊天よ、あふるるみ恵みを与え給え。

太陽のように暖かく
大地のように力づよく
月のように美しく
人間をより向上させるために、また、
富と栄光とを増し加えるために、

この聖所に於て、平和が不和に打ち勝ち、無欲が貪欲を征服し、誠意ある言葉が虚偽を克服し、尊敬が侮辱に勝つことを得せしめ給え。

我々の心に歓喜を与え、我々の魂を高め、我々の肉体に栄光を与え給え。

宇宙の大霊であり、大光明、大活動体にまします尊天、

我らをしてみもとに集まり、礼拝し、御心に近づく者に、

新しき力と栄ある光とを与え給わんことを。

すべては尊天にてまします 七反

The Prayer to Sonten:
Reiki people will notice the kanji 'Rei' as in Reiki, and the kanji for Dai Ko Myo, which is used in Reiki Master classes.

INFORMATION OFFICE: CABLE CAR

VISITORS NOT WISHING TO HIKE the vertical height of the mountain can take the cable car from the Information Office. This eliminates about 400 feet of climbing out of the 525 feet from the front gate to the main temple or the 771 feet to the top of the trail. Taking the cable car does by-pass some interesting sites, most notably the Yuki shrine, the most sacred Shinto site on the mountain. In the main room of the Information Office, tickets can be purchased at the Kiosk for the cable car. The cost is 100 yen ($1 US). After purchasing the ticket, go to the room off to the right and wait for the next car to arrive. Starting at 8:18 a.m. cars leave every 15-20 minutes. The last car leaves at 4:47 p.m. from September 1–May 31. From June 1–August 31 they leave at 5:17 p.m. This schedule is posted in the main room. Those who wish to visit the mountain outside of these times will have to walk. During most of the year, the cable car is a time (and effort) saving option, however, during busy holidays and foliage season, large numbers of people take the cable car, and the wait can be up to an hour long.

When the cable car arrives, notice that it is built at the same angle of steepness as the mountain. This type of cable car is called a funicular. Passengers climb the stairs within the car and sit level. A cable is used to raise and lower the cars because the slope is too steep for wheels to grip. Funiculars like this have been used all over the world, including Athens, Los Angeles, Quebec, Paris, and nearby Mt. Hiei. There are even funicular fan clubs. Kurama's funicular was installed in 1957. The ride is quick, taking only a few minutes. During the train ride, the (Japanese) announcement invites the visitor to breathe in the healthy energy of Kurama Mountain, and mentions Sonten, Kurama's chief deity. When getting out of the cable car and heading into the Upper Cable Car station, there is a place where the machinery that runs the cable car can be seen.

(Text continues as if the visitor is not taking the cable car. Please go to the Upper Cable Car Pagoda, page 44, if you take the cable car, to continue your tour.)

The Kurama Mountain cable car.

Kurama Mountain's funicular cable car is designed to climb the steep slope.

Kɪ Note

ENERGY FROM THE CABLE CAR: The swift rise of the cable car offers a chance to notice how the energy shifts from the lower areas of the mountain, which are raised-seabed, to the higher areas of the mountain which are more volcanic in origin. The energy changes in frequency. Some also discern differences between the energy to the left and to the right of the car. All of the paths and sites of Kurama Mountain are on the left side of the train (assuming you are facing up). To the right is Kurama's wilderness nature preserve.

REIKI NOTE: Some say Mikao Usui may have received Reiki while meditating under one of these waterfalls.

参拝記念

勝馬山内の諸堂や施設を
維持するためにご協力いただき
ありがとうございました
そのお礼として
ケーブルカーを
片道ご利用して
いただきます
この花びらを
係員に呈示して
ご乗車ください

Cable Car ticket.

Looking down the tracks from the cable car.

Waterfalls, Pools and Torii

I F THE VISITOR DOES NOT TAKE THE CABLE CAR and continues up the path, she or he next sees a small path parallel-
ing the access road, to the right. On that path, the visitor encounters Kurama Mountain's two small waterfalls, a small koi
fish pond and several small temple buildings. The rocks in these
lower areas of the mountain are much older than the rocks
near the summit. Japan is an ancient seabed through which
now ancient volcanoes once thrust up. These waterfall features
are actually volcanic springs, diverted through a cement culvert to fall on the rocks below. There is an ancient Japanese esoteric ritual of standing under such waterfalls during the winter, sometimes for hours, and letting the cold-water strike the
top of the head. It is said to both toughen the practitioner, and
to bring on an experience of *satori* or awakening enlightenment. The water flow of these springs is not constant. Every
few minutes the water flow changes, strengthening, receding
to a trickle or even pulsing. The upper waterfall is dedicated to
Maõ-son, whose figure appears at the top. There are a number
of stone torii near these pools, indicating that this is a Shinto
as well as Buddhist site. Many of the torii on Kurama have little stones on top. Small children (and not so small ones) toss
stones into the air to try to get them to land on top for luck,
or to make a wish come true.

The middle temple (without a waterfall) is dedicated to Dakini and Inari. Often associated together, Dakini was originally a Hindu goddess and Inari is connected to the magical fox spirit or kitsune.[1] The temple beside the upper waterfall is dedicated to Keyepo Gansha, the teacher of Yoshitsune, the famous samurai hero raised on Kurama Mountain. The teacher, this version of the legend tells, was the King of the Tengu. It says he used to live in the Ichijo Street and Horikawa river area in Kyoto, and had the ability of fortune-telling. Another source refers to this small temple as Kiitsuhogen-sha or Kiichihogen-sha, and that it is connected to Kiitsu (Kiichi) Hogen, another individual said to be the teacher of Yoshitsune.[2]

KI NOTE

WATERFALL: Even standing near the upper Maō-son waterfall for 10 to 20 minutes or more is a powerful meditation experience. The sound and pattern of water can be mesmerizing. There is also a sense of chi/ki descending from the heights above, directly into the crown chakra. Visually, there is an odd hole between the roots of one of the trees hugging the cliff, and something that looks like a figure sleeping inside.

The lower waterfall.

The Dakini and Inari shrines.

Yuki: Oratory, Tree, Shrines

THE NEXT SERIES OF BUILDINGS is the Yuki shrine, the most powerful Shinto shrine on Kurama Mountain. The visitor leaves the road to walk up the stairway through the oratory building and up into the main shrine. The oratory would traditionally be used as a place for worshippers to pray and listen to services, however this one is seldom used today because of its age and historic value. This oratory or Wari-Haiden is officially designated an important Japanese cultural property. The structure was moved here on September 9, 940 A.D. from the Imperial Palace to protect the city from evil influences traditionally associated with the north. Toyotomi Hideyori, son of the famed military leader Hideyoshi, reconstructed the oratory in 1610 A.D. Many of the stone stairs leading up through the oratory have indentations created by centuries of use by pilgrims' feet.

Family Shrines

Along the stairway are a number of small family shrines. These are places for the family members to come pray and leave offerings.

The Wari-Haiden or
Oratory of the Yuki shrine.

Kami Tree

These trees, and many of the other large trees on Kurama Mountain are a conifer called Cryptomeria Japonica, commonly called Japanese Cedar, or in Japanese "hinõki". The lumber is often used for Noh theatre masks and for sacred architecture. The largest of the three at the Yuki shrine has a trunk more than six feet across and is eight hundred years old.

A sacred
Kami Tree.

KI NOTE

KAMI TREE: A powerful place to experience the ki of this area is right on the path, just a few feet away from the trunk of the main Kami tree. Looking up, see the place where the three trees meet. The mountain ki energy is concentrated at this point and showers down on the passersby, most of whom are too focused on the stairs to even notice. Sitting on the stairs allows for a pleasant rest and view of the Oratory roof. When sitting for some minutes, however, the visitors are likely to experience a huge amount of ki cascading onto their heads. Small adjustments in exactly where to sit on the stair will produce differences in the amount and location of the ki.

Many of the most powerful energy spots on Kurama are near, but not exactly at, the various temples and shrines. Visitors should pay attention to what they feel. Also pay attention to the effects that the geography and nearby surroundings have on the quality and quantity of energy produced.

Yuki Shrine: Main Shrine

THE MAIN YUKI SHRINE AREA consists of several buildings and a spring. To the left of the stairs is the sales building and attached to it a storage area. Half hidden in the corner is a sacred spring. The building across from the stairs is the actual Yuki shrine. As a Shinto site, the gods of the Yuki shrine are considered to be not only in the shrine, but in the area surrounding it. The area behind the shrine has marvelous positive energy, as does the area in the trees above the shrine. Shinto gods are not considered to have a specific form, but just to be the god of a place or a thing.

Shinto is very different from Buddhism, but the two have co-existed in Japan since Buddhism's entry into Japan in the mid 500's. Shinto is a nature-based religion. It considers that certain locations, trees, springs, and even ancestors have special energy. These special energies or *kami* can be asked to intercede on behalf of the petitioner. Shinto focuses on the sacredness of nature, on self-purification and on respecting the natural world. On the side of the shrine are large casks of sake. Sake is often given as an offering, both in formal offerings in the shrine and also informally by shrine visitors. One may find full cups of sake left at the shrines. Sake originated in the third century, and was offered to the gods after each harvest. It is made of rice water and the enzymes to ferment it.

On the ends of the timbers of the main shrine are animal-like guardians called Komainu. Komainu means literally Korean Dog. They can have different forms. Komainu can be found protecting both Shinto shrines and Buddhist temples. On one of the shrine buildings, there is also an odd sign full of numbers. This sign tells visitors which years of age are especially unlucky. According to tradition, there are several unlucky periods called

Yakudoshi in each person's life, lasting three years of which the middle year is the most unlucky. To offset the unlucky years, the visitor is supposed to say extra prayers to the gods and visit many temples and shrines. The left three columns are the years for men, the right three columns are for women. The 16 in the document title refer to the year 2004, known in Japan as Heisei 16, the 16th year of the Heisei emperor. Traditionally, the Japanese consider themselves to be a one-year old when born, so the 'unluckiest' years for men are 24, 41, and 60. And, 18, 32, 36 and 60 are unlucky for women. The kanji (Chinese characters) and numbers above the large number in each square indicate the Japanese year of birth.

Ema Prayer plaques for sale at the Yuki shrine.
The courtyard of the Yuki shrine, and sales building.
The main building is just to the right of the picture.

Visitors can buy cloth brocade charms called omamori and wooden prayer plaques called ema at the Yuki shrine (and a different collection of them at the main temple). Prayers are written on the wooden plaques and left at the shrine. They are periodically burned to release the energy to the gods. Visitors buy and take home the brocade charms that are blessed by a priest of the temple or shrine. They are for different purposes such as: health, good grades, traffic safety and good luck.

To pray in front of the Yuki shrine, the visitor should bow, clap twice, pray quietly, clap again, and bow. The bows are to show respect. The clapping twice invites the gods of heaven and earth to hear the prayer, the clap at the end indicates to the gods the prayer is finished.

Close-up of the Yuki shrine's guardian.

Main building of the Yuki shrine.

Jizõ Shrine

To the right of the road, just past the Yuki shrine, is the Jizõ shrine. Jizõ is the guardian deity of children, pregnant women, travelers and firemen. Jizõ is one of the most popular Bodhisattvas (enlightened beings) in Japan. Jizõ searches the Six Buddhist Realms of Existence for lost souls and rescues them. Jizõ is typically portrayed as a bald, smiling monk, carrying a Buddhist pilgrim staff in one hand and a wish-fulfilling jewel in the other. Jizõ is a popular deity in Tendai Buddhism. Kurama Mountain was Tendai Buddhist before 1949, when the Kurama Kõkyõ sect was started to run the temple.

One will notice on the altar cloths which adorn this temple, the original clockwise version of the swastika or Man-ji. This symbol has represented the creative forces of the universe in Buddhism for millennia. Although originally a Buddhist symbol, the Nazi's used the reversed version to represent their beliefs in destruction. Jizõ is an appropriate patron for healers and others who believe it is their mission to help people find a way out of their own hell and into wholeness.

Jizõ Shrine: Jizõ is the guardian deity of children, travelers and firemen.

MONUMENT TO YOSHITSUNE

To THE LEFT OF THE ROAD, one can look up and see a monument to Yoshitsune. (Yo-shi-tsu-ne) This is the first of many places on the mountain dedicated to one of Japan's most famous Samurai war generals. Yoshitsune grew up on Kurama, (1159-1169) and is said to have learned martial arts here under the training of the Tengu before leaving to seek his fortune at the age of sixteen. The platform where the monument sits was originally the site of the small temple where Yoshitsune lived.

The story of Yoshitsune has also become a successful Japanese television series produced by NHK, based on a historical novel by Tomiko Miyao. Many of Kurama's visitors with an interest in Japanese history, Noh plays, and martial arts visit the mountain to see where Yoshitsune's legend began.

The mountain is full of sites where Yoshitsune, often referred to by his boyhood name of Ushiwaka-maru, lived, slept, drank water, practiced swordmanship, and even measured his height before leaving the mountain to seek his destiny.

The Yoshitsune Monument marks the spot where the 11th-century samurai hero once lived.

WINDING PATH

THE PATH BEGINS TO MAKE HAIRPIN TURNS climbing up the mountain. The Japanese name for this part of the trail is Tsuzura-ori or winding path. Seishōnagon (or Sei Shōnagon) was an eminent female essayist in the 11th-century Kyoto court. Her *Pillowbook* is still a widely read Japanese literature classic. The Kurama Mountain brochure quotes her: "The road to Kurama is a winding path; at a glance it appears quite near, but it is quite far." Seishōnagon was one of the ladies-in-waiting to the empress Sadako during the last decade of the 10th-century, as was her nemesis Murasaki Shikibu, who wrote another Japanese literature classic *The Tale of Genji*; some scenes of which are also set on Kurama Mountain. The two constantly vied for popularity and hated each other, but between them they painted a picture of the court life of that period.

DISTANCE POSTS

Kurama is located only seven miles from the Imperial Palace in Kyoto. Its modest height and cool, summer breezes made it a popular destination for nobility during Kyoto's hot, humid summers. Eight 'distance' markers allowed visitors to gauge how far they had come from the front gate to the main temple. The shapes of the top of these markers and the Sanskrit characters are based on the Five States of Buddhism. The onion top symbolizes emptiness, the cup symbolizes air, the roof symbolizes fire, the sphere symbolizes water and the cube symbolizes earth.

3-RINGED STATUE

The very modern looking 3-ringed statue is in sharp contrast to the traditional look of everything else on the mountain. The central peak of the statue represents Mt. Meru, the home of the gods in the *Lotus Sutra*, and by implication Kurama Mountain.

The statue is titled (in Japanese) "Love, Light and Power", which are the qualities attributed to Kurama's trinity of deities: Kannon the Love of the Moon, Bishamonten the Light of the Sun, and Maõ-son to the Power of Earth.

The tree shrine beside the creek is dedicated to Ebisu, the Lucky God of Commerce.

KI NOTE

HAIRPIN ENERGIES There are many great energies at the hairpin turns of the path. Use your hands to scan and greet the natural energies of trees, rocks and water on Kurama Mountain, and certainly, explore how the energies of the different spots differ in power and character. The more energy work the visitor does on the way up the mountain, the more focused she or he will be on the energy frequency-ranges of the mountain and, therefore, the stronger an energetic experience one will have. More sensitive visitors should minimize the amount of energy play they do on the way up the mountain to avoid getting overloaded too early on the trip.

3 Ringed Statue: Each ring symbolizes the deities of Kurama and their qualities: power, love and light.

Camellia hedges

Chumon Gate

O N THE RIGHT SIDE OF THE PATH, just past the three-ringed statue, are inviting shrines dedicated to Ebisu, the lucky god of commerce, and Daikokuten, the lucky god of prosperity. The mountain's energy is very strong here, making it a lovely place to meditate for a few moments. There are several benches to sit on. The rock retaining wall was rebuilt in 2004.

Chumon Gate

The Chumon or 'middle gate' straddles the path at the next sharp curve. Buddhist temples typically have a main gate and a middle gate before reaching the main temple. There are a number of picturesque spots on this part of the mountain, wooden bridges, rock retaining walls, and angular architecture. To the left of the Chumon Gate are a number of piles of quarried granite, used for various construction projects. The sign (in Japanese) advises visitors to leave the rocks alone, as poisonous snakes like to sun themselves on the sun-warmed stones.

Heart designs decorate Chumon Gate.

Chumon Gate

この石置場には
マムシがいますので
ご注意ください

This sign warns of poisonous snakes dwelling near Chumon Gate.

Empress's Resting Place

At the hairpin curve of the path is a little alcove with a bench and a marker. This site was created as a nice resting place for the Empress Teimei, who was the wife of the Taisho emperor and mother to Emperor Hirohito (Showa). She visited the mountain in 1924 (Taisho 13).

Donor Posts

There are numerous donor stones lining the path. The stone posts on either side of the path date from the 1920's. They are carved with the donation amount of 100 Yen ($1 US) and the donor's name. Today the value of the yen is about a penny. However, during the 1920's, the equivalent of a paperback novel would cost one yen. A hundred yen was a substantial amount of money, equivalent to hundreds of dollars today.

Signs in Three Directions

The path comes to a place where signs (in Japanese) point to three directions. The south sign leads back to the front gate of the temple, the north sign leads to the upper station for the cable car, and the west sign points to the path continuing up the mountain.

The path winds passed this tiny temple to the lucky god of long life, Jurojin.

NOTE

The next page will start as if the visitor is coming from the cable car station. If you are not coming from the cable car either skip the next few pages and start again at the Lower Courtyard, or proceed down the north path (which will curve east) until you get to the upper cable car station.

3-way sign: The crossroads of upper cable car, main temple and entrance

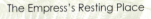

The Empress's Resting Place

Upper Cable Station Pagoda

V ISITORS WHO WALK UP THE MOUNTAIN instead of taking the cable car typically turn west at the three-way sign pictured on the last page, and miss the sites pictured on the next few pages. If the visitor instead goes north at the three-way sign, and follows the path to the upper cable car station, she or he will then be able to see these sites as well.

Cable Car Station (not shown)

The upper cable car station has a number of beautiful photographs of various shrines and temples on the mountain. Tickets to take the cable car down can be purchased for 100 Yen ($1 US). To the right of the ticket window is a window that looks down onto the cable car machinery.

Tahōtō Pagoda

Outside the upper cable car station is the Tahōtō Pagoda. The original pagoda was next to the main temple, and burned down in 1814. A new pagoda was rebuilt on this site as part of the temple's 1200th birthday celebration in 1970.

Tahōtō Pagoda was erected as part of Kurama's 1200th birthday celebration.

Ki Note

PATHWAY ENERGY: The energy of the mountain is particularly strong in this place, as the ki energy ascends and descends the steep ravine. There is a sense of deep quiet. Noticing the changes in how the area 'feels' can help connect the visitor more deeply to the sacred energy of the mountain. Different people will feel these changes in different areas of their bodies, often in their hands, third eye or heart. Also experiment with slowly turning around to help determine if there is more energy on one side than the other. It is apparent that the mountain is very steep, especially noticeable above and below the path. One can also see very large trees along this path.

Pathway near the Upper Cable Car Station.

THE BUDDHA OF THE FUTURE

BUDDHISM AND SHINTO HAVE EXISTED SIDE-BY-SIDE for so long that many sites on the mountain are a mix of both. The temple to the Buddha of the Future is a good example. One passes through a Shinto stone *torii* to go into the temple. The Buddha of the Future is Miroku Bosatsu, whose Sanskrit name is Maitreya. This being will be born 5,670,000,000 years after the death of the historical Buddha, who lived about 2500 years-ago. Buddhists believe in a long-term future! The Buddha of the Future is not a solemn figure. Miroku Bosatsu is known as the friendly, loving or laughing Buddha. Before he became fully enlightened, he would stand outside the gates of the city and meditate on lovingkindness. His contemplation was so powerful that those who passed by experienced the great love of the universe. He is known for leading people towards enlightenment by encouraging spiritual discipline, concentration and wisdom. Some sources state that Hotei, the Laughing Buddha and Chinese God of Luck with the big belly, is an incarnation of Miroku Bosatsu.

Temple to the Buddha of the Future.

KI NOTE

LOVE MEDITATION: Spend several minutes contemplating the joyful, divine love of the universe for all beings.

Signs Point Out Three Directions (Revisited)

Continue along the path to the place where the signs point in three directions. Take the path to the west. (The path to the north goes to the cable car.) This path opens up into the lower courtyard, and stairs climb upward.

Stairway

The blue-black and yellow-red stone used in the stairway was quarried on Kurama Mountain. The sign beside the mountain says that the stone is seven million-years-old. This is also some of the youngest stone on Kurama Mountain! Kurama granite is valued for its color variation and pattern. There are a number of stone masons in Kurama village who craft lanterns and other garden art from these special stones.

Ki Note

KURAMA STONE BOUNCE: Energetically the Kurama stone has a very different quality than the imported grey stone used elsewhere on the mountain. People with strong ki energy in their hands can stand and 'bounce' the energy from their hand onto earth and get an almost radar-like sense of the energy 'bouncing' back. Different surfaces have different degrees of 'bounce'. It is easiest to test this in an area where there are different kinds of surfaces next to each other, such as grey granite, Kurama granite, gravel and earth. All of these surfaces are available near the stairway.

PRACTICAL NOTE: MYSTERY RESTROOMS: There are restrooms in the same little plaza as the stone stairway. I have labeled these 'mystery' restrooms, because they are labeled with the Japanese kanji for men and women. Guideless non-Japanese reading visitors may need to wait a few minutes to see someone go in or out to determine which is which. The south side (closest to edge) is for women and the north side (closest to the climb for the mountain) is for men. Visitors feeling a need to use the restroom 'soon' should take advantage of this rest stop because this is the last restroom before a long stairway, the Buddha and the main temple area. These are Japanese-style 'squatter' restrooms, and having your own toilet paper, hand sanitizer and handkerchief is recommended.

Snail with shells about 2" across evolved from sea snails prevalent when Japan was ocean bottom.

The Rest Area.

A stairway made of rock quarried on Kurama Mountain.

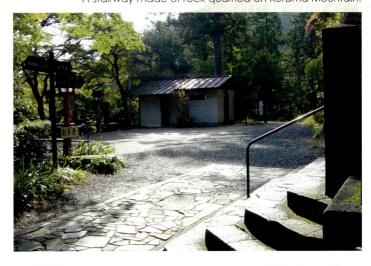

Benzaiten: Goddess of the Arts

There is a temple to the left of the stairway. It is dedicated to Benzaiten, the Goddess of eloquence, music, fortune and art. She is usually depicted playing a mandolin-like instrument called a biwa. Benzaiten, also called Benten, is one of the many Buddhist deities that originated in India and migrated across Asia. Benzaiten is known as Sarasvati in India. She is the only female deity in the Gods of Luck, seen in both China and Japan.

Library
(not open to the public)

Stairway to the Library.

This building is to the left of the stairs, half-hidden by a wooden fence. It was once used as a reception hall for the visit of Empress Teimei, who was the wife of the Taisho Emperor, reigning from 1912-1926. The building is now used as a library and a writing room for holy texts. The Empress was the mother of Emperor Hirohito. She disagreed with him over Japan's entry into WWII. She died in 1951. This type of Japanese architecture known as the Shinden style was popular with the upper classes during the Heian period. (794-1185 A.D.)

Ki Note

PRAYING TO BENZAITEN: According to the sign, prayer to Benzaiten brings good luck, virtue, intelligence, treasure, fortune and accomplishment.

Shrine to Benzaiten, The Goddess of Music and Arts.

The Writing Room was originally used as a reception hall for the Empress Teimei.

REFRESHMENT ROOM:
WASHING YOUR MIND

T HE NEXT BUILDING IS TO THE RIGHT of the stairs. The first floor contains a refreshment room called "Washing your Mind" (Senshintei). The second floor of the building is a separate exit off the path and it is described on the next page. The sign there invites the visitor:

Since old days, to visit Kurama, people used to have to climb, step-by-step, up the main road called Tsuzura-ori (winding path), which is the route that looks close but is long. When they have almost arrived, their legs were tired and they felt thirsty, then they needed to rest at this tea place. After moistening their throats and calming their feelings, they would visit the main hall. Now the tea place is located close to the Buddha of Tenpõrin-dõ, and is called Senshintei 'Washing your Mind', and offers a place to relax. At the moment of your visit, please have a rest here and then visit the main hall refreshed in your body and soul. May you receive the energy from Sonten during your visit to Kurama Temple."

The refreshment room is closed Mondays, unless it is a holiday weekend, in which case it will be closed on Tuesday. It opens around 11:30 a.m. and closes in the mid-afternoon. It also sells Kurama chopsticks, wooden rice spatulas, ice cream and other packaged Japanese snacks. The refreshment room serves tea, and a number of seasonal Japanese beverages. The drink menu is translated into English.

There is a restaurant on the first floor of Tenpõrin-dõ.

PRACTICAL NOTE

VENDING MACHINE Outside the restaurant, and open even if the restaurant is closed, is a vending machine with small boxes of tea and juice. This is the only such vending machine in the temple part of the mountain.

TENPŌRIN-DŌ

DRAGON PURIFICATION SHRINE

The Dragon Fountain at the Purification Shrine.

Next on the path is a Shinto purification shrine. Here one purifies oneself before sitting in front of the Buddha, or before going up to the main temple. The shrine was updated in 2003 with an elegant brass dragon that pours water into the basin. Since Shinto and Buddhism have intimately combined throughout Japan, one purifies oneself at this Shinto purification site before going to sit before the Buddha, or heading up to the main temple.

ENTERING TENPŌRIN-DŌ

At the purification shrine, it is recommended that instead of heading straight up to the main temple complex, you turn and walk into the building to the right. This is actually the second floor of the refreshment room building. This building is called Tenpōrin-dō, which means "Lotus Wheel Hall." To enter, walk around to the south side of the building. The next few pages describe all of the things that can be found in the hall.

HOW TO REMOVE SHOES

Shoes are left outside.

Japanese are very serious about where shoes can and cannot be worn, especially at temples. It is not uncommon for visitors to be yelled at for doing it incorrectly. The visitor should stand on the concrete with shoes facing away from the building, heels touching the platform. Remove your shoes and leave them on the concrete. Only bare or stocking feet should touch the wooden platform. Purses, backpacks and coats can be brought inside and left on the floor while the visitor is inside. Visitors are asked to not take pictures.

Worshipping Inside the Hall

Worship here is a very personal thing. Visitors may do the ritual most meaningful to them. Spending time in meditation here, or just unobtrusively sitting, especially during busy times, is a marvelous way to quietly see how people worship.

Purification shrine outside Buddha Hall.

THE AMIDA BUDDHA

DOMINATING THE ROOM IS a twelve-foot-tall statue of the Amida Buddha. The Amida Buddha is known for helping all souls reach enlightenment regardless of their level of intellect or knowledge. The name Amida means Infinite Light or Infinite Life.[3] Only the head of the Buddha is immediately visible. In front of it is an altar platform that runs the width of the building, with a central access stairway. This particular statue is quite young by Japanese standards, having been made in Middle Edo period (18th century). The Buddha was made in Kamakura style (13th -14th century) in that it has shining eyes. The eyes of this Buddha are also unusual in that they look down upon the worshippers, rather than out at a distant horizon. The hand positions of the Buddha and other deities are called mudras, and they have special meanings.

This Buddha's hands are in the Vitarka Mudra, with the thumb touching the first finger of the hand. One hand is raised facing towards the visitors, the other hand is in the same mudra, but placed in the lap. This hand position indicates the gesture of consciousness, or the gesture of knowledge. It is often used when a statue is proclaiming a teaching. The three extended fingers symbolize lethargy, activity, and balance / harmony. The closed circle of index finger and thumb depict the union of the individual soul with the world soul.

KI NOTE

SITTING BEFORE THE BUDDHA: This is one of my favorite places to come and sit on Kurama Mountain. This Buddha's energy is calm, and I often feel a soft pressure against my third eye, and sometimes over my whole body. The energy feels like a gentle green mist or wave.

Amida Buddha

SITTING BEFORE THE BUDDHA

It is permissible to crawl under the stairway and sit directly in front of the Buddha. A Buddhist priest/friend, and later the temple attendant who often sits in this room confirmed this. In the privacy of this little alcove beneath the stairs, the visitor can meditate without being seen by most of the other visitors. From this position, the whole statue can be seen through the vertical rails. A five colored rope ties the hand of the Buddha to the rails trailing into the alcove. Touching the rope (tied to the Buddha's hand) is like touching the hand of the Buddha. The Buddha also seems to change expression, at different times looking peaceful, reproachful or pleased. One of the temple attendants reported that a black tear appeared in one of his eyes on the day of September 11, 2001 when the terrorist attacks occurred in the U.S. The sign attached to the rails in the alcove beneath the stair, requests that visitors sit here to contemplate the nature of the Buddha and give thanks. It asks visitors not to pray for help or ask questions about the future at this particular location.

THE REVOLVING LOTUS WHEEL

THIS SMALL WHEEL NEAR THE MIDDLE of the room is over 850 years-old and called the Tenporin, or the revolving lotus wheel. A Buddhist priest created the wheel. He wrote (by hand) the names of 60,000 priests (hogo), and put the names inside it. The followers of Amida Buddhism believe that by endlessly reciting the mantra "Namu Amida Butsu" ("I take refuge in the Amida Buddha"), it is enough to break the bonds of negative karma. Spinning the wheel while saying the mantra is supposed to have the effect of having all 60,000 priests reciting this mantra.

THE HEALING STATUE

The reddish-brown statue to the left of the doorway is of Binzuru. He was a doctor, said to be a disciple (arhat) of the historical Buddha. Others say that the statue is actually of Yakushi Nyorai, the Buddha of Healing and Medicine. Regardless of its exact identity, people with illnesses or injuries, and loved ones of the sick, seek it out at the Buddhist temple. They seek healing from the statue by making an offering, saying a prayer and then rubbing the statue in the same area on its body where their illness occurs.

THE KURAMA KŌKYŌ AND THE TEMPLE FOUNDER

To the left of the Amida Buddha statue, in a small alcove, is a statue of the founder of the Kurama Kōkyō sect, Kōun Shigaraki. The Kurama Kōkyō sect has run Kurama Temple since 1949. They consider themselves to be the stewards of the mountain. The founder's daughter, Konin Shigaraki is

Kurama's current high priestess. She took over after his death in 1972 and is eighty-two years-old. (2006)

MORE DETAILS ABOUT THE HALL

The golden chandelier-like structure hanging from the ceiling is a symbolic representation of the umbrella held over the historical Buddha to protect him from the elements. Here it hangs above where the priest sits. Behind the Buddha statue on the wall are many golden disks. The names of various do-

Platform at the Amida Buddha shrine.

nors who helped restore the hall appear on them. The large rope of meditation beads is a decoration that appears at this and other temples, and is used for group chanting in some Buddhist rituals. There is also a hall called Tenpōrin-dō at the Enryakuji Temple on Mt. Hiei, indicating Kurama's Tendai Buddhist roots.

Worshippers rub this statue for healing.

THE MAIN TEMPLE COMPLEX

Looking out from the courtyard.

Leaving the Amida Buddha Temple area and continuing up the stairs, one reaches the main temple complex. The main temple complex is about two-thirds of the distance to the top of the mountain. For most visitors this is the main destination and once they explore it, they will then head back. Around an open, central plaza, there are a number of buildings and points of interest in the complex. The sites will be covered from right to left, starting with sites near the front/south and working toward the north/back.

Picnic building

The first building, to the right of the stairs, is a rest station for visitors who may choose to picnic inside. There may even be a heater there on cold days.

Bronze Lanterns

A pair of these bronze lamps stand in the main courtyard.

There are two large bronze lanterns in the plaza. They are lit at dusk just like the other lamps on the mountain. On their octagonal bases are the traditional, mythic, beast guardians of the four directions. North is the black turtle and snake. West is the white tiger. South is the phoenix, and East is the dragon. The deity pictured on the lanterns is Bishamonten.

Courtyard.

Picnic building where visitors are invited to eat and relax.

AKAI-GOHŌ-ZENJIN SHRINE

P AST THE PICNIC BUILDING is the trellised arbor way that provides summer shade and leads visitors to the Akai Shrine in the northeast corner of the complex. The shrine is a building that shelters a sacred spring. Many ema plaques are placed on the outside of the shrine. Legend says that in the late ninth century, two large mystical snakes attacked a priest at that very spot. The priest killed the male snake, but the female snake surrendered. She promised the priest that if spared, she would guard the spring and ensure that the water would always be clear and good. This legend is the basis of the Takekiri ceremony in which two groups of priests compete in cutting up bamboo poles (representing the snakes) every June 20. The water at this spot is considered to be sacred. Visitors pump water from the well into the buckets, and then fill their own bottles that they have brought for this purpose. The water is said to have healing properties. (The well may run dry at certain times of the year.)

The sign next to the well translates: "If you take some of this water, remember... This water belongs to the Buddha, it is sacred. A single drop is a gift from heaven, don't waste it. Think of washing the body as a heart purification. This water from Sonten is a protection from harm."

Outer shrine wall with ema prayer requests and paper cranes.

Wisteria shades the entry to the Akai shrine Akai shrine.

A thousand years ago, a snake agreed to protect this well.

SACRED STONE

To the left of the entry stairs, overlooking the mountains at the edge of the plaza, is an area cordoned-off with a sacred rope (Shimenawa).[4] A large flat stone, about 5 by 3 feet, is located in the middle. Many visitors who photograph the beautiful views barely notice this powerful stone. The stone was originally the cover to a storage crypt for more than 200 sacred writings (sutras) located behind the main temple. The name of the stone is Flying Cloud base (Sho un dai). Another source refers to it as the rock where Maõ-son landed on earth.[5]

KI NOTE

SCAN THE SACRED STONE: The energy of the stone is quite strong, possibly emanating from the sutras once stored below it!

This sacred stone once covered a crypt of sacred writings or sutras.

CENTRAL MANDALA

T HE CENTERPIECE OF THE PLAZA is the mandala, inset in the courtyard between the Main Temple and the Sacred Stone. The mandala is about twenty feet in diameter. At its center is a triangle within a hexagon. This is surrounded by three concentric circles, made up of triangles, within a larger square with triangles in the corner. A tiny double triangle at the edge of the outer circle points to true north. This mandala marks the spot where the temple's main spirit deity came down from heaven to look towards the capital of Kyoto, just on the other side of the hills to the south.

KI NOTE

STANDING ON THE MANDALA: The traditional power point is in the center triangle of the mandala, facing the energy of the main temple. This is where the energies of heaven and earth mix. A less traditional, but very powerful energy point is on the stairs of the temple, facing the central triangle inside the mandala. Kurama's energy cascades off the roof, and also flows from the sacred stone and mandala. Some say the energy varies with the time of the day. Some energy practitioners recommended scanning the energy at noon. The author felt a greater shift at sunset and suspects another would occur at dawn. A friend said "I was there, after Wesak, and the energy was exhilarating! We lingered."

Side view of the mandala in front of the main temple.

The mandala in front of the main temple.

OUTSIDE THE MAIN TEMPLE

O VER THE CENTURIES FIRE has been a major destructive force, destroying much of Japan's traditional wood architecture, which is (hopefully) then rebuilt. Kurama Mountain has had many fires. An individual who has lived in Kurama village all of his life said a fire destroyed Kurama's main temple only a few months

Main Temple.

before the bombs were dropped on Hiroshima in WWII. Another source confirmed that the Okunoin burned in January of 1945. The main hall and several other buildings burned in April of that same year. The temple was last rebuilt in the 1970's.

THE TEMPLE'S GUARDIAN TIGERS

Bronze spiral tigers, the guardian statues of the temple, are to either side of the main temple stairs. Kurama's founder had the vision of Bishamonten, that led to the founding of Kurama Temple on the year, day and hour of the tiger. According to the Chinese zodiac based calendar, this occurs once every twelve

Komainu (right side) with mouth open.

years. Thus Kurama's temple guardians are tigers. These temple guardian animals are called Komainu which means Korean Dog. A temple may use other animals, but in the case of Kurama, it's the tiger. Komainu can be found guarding both Buddhist temples and Shinto shrines. While the animals chosen to guard a Buddhist temple vary, the right-side guardian will always have its mouth open, and the left-side guardian will always have its mouth closed. Few know why. The key is to pronounce it, right-to-left, the way the Japanese was traditionally read. The open mouth is Ah and the closed mouth is umm. Together, they make the sacred Buddhist mantra A-um, more commonly spelled Om. The Om is considered to be the sound of the universe. It contains all opposites, the beginning and the end of time, in-ward and outward energies. A Japanese friend described it as

The author is standing by the closed mouth tiger.

Ah is the shape of the mouth when the baby is born and the um is the shape of the mouth when the old person dies, there-fore Ah-um means the whole life of the person from the birth to the death. Visitors who walk up to the temple are walking up in between these two great poles of existence.

THE THREE DOORWAYS

There are three doorways at the front of the main temple. This is to allow each of the temple deities to 'shine outward' and send their energy into the universe.

View from the steps of the Main Temple.

KI NOTE

WALKING PAST THE DOORWAYS: Visitors may wish to close their eyes and walk past the three doorways to see if they can sense the energy emanating from each one. The quality of energy seems to vary depending on the time of day, the number of visitors, and perhaps the time of year.

INSIDE THE MAIN TEMPLE

ENTERING AND LEAVING THE TEMPLE

To enter the temple, walk around to the right-hand entrance (East). It is polite to always enter the temple from the right and leave from the left. If you choose to go into the basement of the temple, also enter from the right-side and depart from the left.

THE MAIN TEMPLE ROOM

All visitors are welcome in the concrete walking area inside the main temple. The carpeted interior worship area is not open to visitors except on special occasions or holidays. Sometimes this area is used for general services, other times for blessings or special offerings. Visitors are welcome to listen from the walking area. Only priests are allowed in the innermost uncarpeted areas of the main room. The daily closing ritual of the temple happens in the late afternoon, complete with chanting and drums. The central image in the back of the worship area is a statue of Bishamonten, brought to the temple from Nara by the temple's founder in 770AD.

The east and west sales areas have different items, although some overlap. Items also vary somewhat from year-to-year. Notable from the eastern sales area are items such as white pillar candles with *The Heart Sutra* (a translation appears later in this book), and a gold-embossed temple crest

The Main Temple.

with the temple's name. Also there are blessed temple charms called *omamori*. Different charms are available for longevity, good luck and traffic-safety. There are also some decorative objects depicting the current or next year's Chinese zodiac animal. Each animal actually represents three things: a year, a single day in a twelve-day cycle, and a two-hour period within a twenty-four hour day. The animals also represent compass directions. The animals are Rat, Ox, Tiger, Rabbit, Dragon, Snake, Horse, Sheep, Monkey, Hen, Dog and Pig.

The west sales area has more books (only in Japanese, unfortunately) about the temple's history, its art treasures and its philosophy. There are also some collections of post cards, and one or two CD's of a famous artist who has performed Koto (a Japanese stringed instrument) concerts at the temple. Journey books are also sold at the temple's west sales area. These blank books, called nokyo-cho, contain a long, continuous sheet of paper folded into book form. At most temples and major shrines, (and at this location) visitors can present an opened journey book, and for 300 yen ($3 US) a priest will inscribe a page with the temple seal, his or her personal seal, and the date. Visitors who cannot read Japanese calligraphy may want to write on the opposing page in their own language, the temple's name, date and personal observations.

Inside Main Temple.   Temple sales area.

BENEATH THE TEMPLE

MOST CASUAL VISITORS NEVER SUSPECT the presence of a sacred room beneath the temple. If you choose to explore it, be discreet and respectful. The room is reached by entering the temple from the east entrance. Turn right, and head down the stairway. The area beneath the temple is almost completely dark. Allow your eyes to adjust. There are florescent light fixtures with switches along the walls, but most visitors prefer the darkness. In this sacred space, please be considerate of worshippers by staying quiet and not using the lights when other visitors may be present.

CANDLELIT ALTAR

After going down the stairs, enter through the curtained-doorway into the dark below. There will be a flickering glow of candles in the darkened hall linking together the up and down stairways. The candles are on an altar. There is an offering box, and a place to burn the special tan colored incense. On the other side of the altar is a glowing cylindrical sign with black Japanese writing. Here is the translation: May we offer superb incense for the deliverance from the small and ordinary Ego (Self) to live with Profound Heaven that is the Universal Soul, Great Light, and Acting Entity, to awake to the True Ego (Self); and for the Prayer of Hair Purification.

Books for sale on Kurama.

Reiki Note

GREAT LIGHT: The kanji for Great Light (Dai Ko Myo) that appears on the round sign below the temple is familiar to most Reiki Masters.

Entrance to the sacred room below
the stairs. Please be discreet and quiet.

Altar below the main temple.

TREASURE PALACE OF URNS

A S THE EYES ADJUST, YOU WILL SEE thousands of small porcelain urns on the shelves. Many assume they contain the ashes of the dead. Instead, they contain locks of hair from the temple parishioners. The room is called the treasure palace because of these urns. The sign pictured below explains:

"This treasure palace simply exemplifies the teaching of Kurama Mountain. All beings, including humankind, are manifestations of Universal Energy and are created by the Universal Life Being. The teachings of Kurama Mountain are: Be grateful at being given life, and take good care of all other lives. Let us live to the fullest in order to improve and evolve our lives as worthy high and profound aspects of the Universal Life Being. Deep inside this treasure palace, three respected deities are enshrined. The purified hair, which represents our lives, is enshrined around the deities. These are not the remains of dead people, but of people representing the teachings above."

Treasure sign discusses the significance of the urns.

Hanging lamps illuminate the path.

BENEATH THE TEMPLE:
The Hidden Gods

URNS ON THEIR SHELVES FORM A PATHWAY that leads into the deepest mystery of the temple. The easiest way to follow the path in the near blackness, is to look up, and follow the dimly-lit lanterns. Visitors should be careful not to disturb the urns or bump into the shelves. Follow the pathway to the back of the room and you'll see the statues of all three of the major deities of Kurama Temple. This is the only place on the mountain where statues of all three deities are on display. From left to right: Maõ-son, Bishamonten, and Kannon (KwanYin). At first, the visitor can see only bits of them, with more details emerging as time passes and the eyes adjust to the dim light. The statues are made of stained wood with gold leaf lines, similar to the statue of Bishamonten in the Information Office by the cable car.

The back of Maõ-son's statue is carved to be the shape of the image of the Õsugi Gongen tree. This thousand-year-old giant Japanese cedar was considered to be an incarnation of the god Maõ-son. The tree was blown over in a typhoon in 1950. The wood from the broken top half has been used to make many artifacts, including these statues. The weathered remainder of the bottom section of the tree still stands near the top of the mountain at Õsugi Gongen. This is also where most Reiki people believe Mikao Usui received the Reiki energy. Maõ-son is portrayed as a stout, middle-aged man, befitting his role as the power of Earth. He has wings, unusual for a Japanese statue, but befitting his origin on the planet Venus and a subsequent flight to the earth. Maõ-son is a deity unique to Kurama Mountain. According to the legend of the mountain, he came to earth to guide the evolution of mankind.

Urns containing the purified hair of temple members.

Bishamonten is the figure in the center. He is portrayed with a tiger or lion's head in his belt to indicate his fierceness. Bishamonten appears in *The Lotus Sutra*, one of Buddhism's most sacred writings. Kurama Temple was founded to honor Bishamonten.

Kannon/ Kwan Yin is one of Japan's most beloved deities. This is the esoteric Senjukannon (thousand-armed Kannon). Each of her arms carries a different object that represents a divine quality and the heads on her crown represent her different aspects. She is associated with compassion, and hearing the cries of all who call out to her for assistance.

Behind the statues a small natural spring drips water. To exit: Take the passageway through the urns to the hallway, then take the stairs on the west side.

The three gods of Kurama Temple: Maō-son, Bishamonten and Kannon.

KŌMYŌSHINDEN

E XITING THE TEMPLE, THE NEXT SMALL BUILDING to the west is the Kōmyōshinden. This temple is open only on busier days. The name of the temple translates as Palace of the Luminous Mind. Inside is Maō-son, portrayed here as a stout, middle-aged man, as befits a God of Earth, with wings, indicating his ability to travel between planets. According to some of the oldest stories on Kurama, his origin is the planet Venus. Other stories associate him with the Kurama Tengu of legend.

An ornate temple gong inside the temple.

Painting of the Kurama Tengu.

Maō-son, depicted here as a stout figure with wings.

ROPED-OFF SQUARE

Between Kōmyōshinden and the Corner Pavilion is a square, roped-off by a sacred rope. This square is used for burning a sacred fire during certain holidays.

CORNER PAVILION

The Corner Pavillion is a place for visitors to sit in the shade. A number of wooden panels, donated by members of the temple, are on display here. One of the panels shows the head of a Tengu, with a stylized fan on either side. The Kurama Tengu are legendary. They are a kind of Japanese goblin with a red face and long nose, known for their prowess in the martial arts. This is a common place for visitors to sit and picnic, especially in good weather. It is also a good place to people watch the other visitors on the plaza. Visitors either sit with their feet dangling over the edge, or leave their shoes on the concrete below.

The Kōmyōshinden. Between the Pavilion and Kōmyōshinden, a roped-off square is used for fire ceremonies.

From south of the pavilion visitors can look down
and see lower levels of the main office.

TEMPLE OFFICE

THE TEMPLE OFFICE (HONBŌ) IS at the western edge of the main temple complex.

OFFICE ROCK GARDEN

In front of the office is a small rock garden. The rocks in the garden symbolize Kurama Mountain. Some of the rocks are from Kurama's ancient seabed formations and contain small fossils of primitive sea creatures; other rocks are volcanic and come from near the mountain top.

THE OFFICE

Most visitors ask questions in the sales area, but more detailed questions or administrative issues are handled here. Only Japanese is spoken. Some of the temple's priests and priestesses live in the lower floors of this building. The lower floors are visible from the south side of the pavilion.

TRAIL HEADING UP

Most visitors don't even notice that the trail continues up the mountain. There is a roofed passageway used by the temple priests that extends from the office building to the main temple. It has a raised wooden floor so they can go from place to place, even in inclement weather, without having to change into and out of sandals. The hiking path to Kibune intersects this passageway near the complex's northwest corner. At this point there is a carefully shaped break in the raised wooden

The Flying Saucer symbolizes the 'heavenly vehicle' that Maō-son used to get to Kurama from Venus.

floor so hikers can go up the trail, but the break is narrow enough that the priests can jump over it on the way to and from the temple.

The majority of visitors do not go any farther than the main temple complex, and simply turn around and go back down to Kurama village. There are signs (in

The path to the top of Kurama exits the main temple complex here.

Japanese), warning visitors to watch out for bears and people asking for money. The author has seen neither of these.

The main office of Kurama temple.

REIKI NOTE

MIKAO USUI: Numerous people (including Arjava Petter and others quite fluent in Japanese) have asked about Mikao Usui, but there is no record of him having been at the temple. There is also no record of the twenty-one day training. A few of the temple staff have learned a little about Reiki from the many visitors who ask about it, but they have no special information or interest in it. Their focus is on the temple's long history, its deities, and its beliefs.

Purification Shrine at Far Side of Temple Complex

T HE PURIFICATION SHRINE, just past the main temple complex at the beginning of the trail, is a great place for visitors who don't intend to go further to get a taste of the less tamed parts of the mountain and to at least get a feel for its energy.

Belfry

As the pathway begins to ascend, a small trail leads sharply up and to the right. Visitors climbing the path will find the temple bell and a beautiful view of the temple complex below. The bell was cast for the temple in 1670. Visitors are welcome to strike the bell by pulling back the wooden log-striker, and releasing it. A Buddhist temple bell has 108 little projecting knobs called chichi near the top, representing the 108 sins recognized by Buddhism. Ringing the bell drives out these evil desires. All over Japan on New Year's Day, such bells are rung 108 times to clear the 108 sins. Near the rim of the bell is a circular lotus design that designates where the bell is supposed to be struck. Logs are used to ring the bell because they are heavy, won't damage the bell, and are easy to replace.

Ki Note

THE WILDS OF KURAMA: The energetic feel of the mountain changes noticeably as one leaves the main temple complex. The energy is noticeably 'wilder.' There are a number of power points in this immediate area. The energy-aware visitor may wish to move around and see which one is strongest. The energy pouring off the eaves is quite strong at this point.

Kurama Temple Bell.

A purification shrine and the path up are visible through this entryway.

KI NOTE

HELPING WOUNDED ENERGIES: I spent time three days in a row at the temple bell in 2002. I sensed that many visitors brought their troubles to the temple and part of their prayer was to leave some of those troubles behind. This means that over the centuries, the temple acquired a build-up of these wounded energies. Sitting near the bell, looking down upon the temple, I felt some of these energies nearby, and I offered to help heal a few by using Reiki. I did three, each day, for three days. They were each different, some felt like sadness, some felt like a lizard-like, or bird-like creature with a broken arm and some felt like people who were lost. On the fourth day I returned, and offered to do some more work. I got this sense of "Thank you, but no! Thanks for showing us what to do, and we'll take it from here..." Every year I return to this point, and see if "they" have anything else for me to do.

Purification Shrine.

Poems and Poets Study

RETURNING TO THE MAIN TRAIL, the visitor next reaches a small plaza with a large modern building. The building is the Kurama Museum, described on the next page. The area outside the museum is dedicated to Akiko and Tekkan Yosano. Akiko Yosano was best known for writing passionate verse and founding the literary journal *Myojo* (Venus.) She was a very important Japanese feminist, who actively promoted the equality of women. Also, Akiko and her husband spoke out against the first Sino-Japanese war (1894-1895), and the nationalistic fervor of the time.

Poems

Just before reaching the museum are two rock monuments. These are engraved with poems about Kurama, written by poet Akiko Yosano (1868-1942), on the right stone, and one by her husband, Tekkan, on the left stone. The rough translations are below.

I feel like meeting you so I come up in this field of flowers (cherry blossoms)

    Then I found an evening moon here

           —Akiko

I found the rock which Yoshitsune used to compare his height on this mountain.

    My heart is still waiting for tomorrow.

          —Kan (Tekkan)

Poet's Study

The small Japanese building to the left of the museum is poetess Akiko Yosanos study, which was moved here in 1976. More artifacts and poems of the Yosano's can be found in the museum.

The famous poets, Akiko and Tekkan Yosano wrote poems about Kurama.

This building was the study of the famous poetess.

Museum.

Reihōden (Museum)

HE MUSEUM IS OPEN FROM 9 a.m. to 4 p.m. It is closed Mondays and holidays, and closed from mid-December through February. Admission is 200 Yen (about $2 US).

First floor: Natural History

To one side of the payment window is a shelf containing a number of books about the mountain and the area (in Japanese). There is also a book about the statues and cultural treasures owned by the temple.

Dominating the foyer is a diorama of the wildlife on Kurama Mountain. The diorama includes stuffed examples of the animals and insects commonly found on the mountain including deer, flying squirrels, owls, and the Japanese raccoon dog called tanuki.

The Geology Exhibit in the main room has examples of the different kinds of rock found on the mountain. Signs explain how Kurama had once been part of an ancient seabed, and thus the rocks farther down the slopes of the mountain are much older than the rocks near the top. There are a number of maps showing the topology and soil structure of the area, and time lines of the mountain's history. Near the center of the room, a scale-model diorama of the mountain shows the topology of the mountain and the location of all of its buildings and trails.

The Biology Exhibit focuses on some of the botany of the mountain, including ferns, grasses and seedpods. There are cases of butterfly and insect collections. These are used by biologists to get a pictorial depiction of the differences between species and individuals of each species. There is also a pictorial depiction of the snails that have evolved on the mountain from being ocean snails when the area was a shallow ocean seabed, to land snails as the mountains arose seven-million years-ago. There is a diorama of the local sea life seven million years ago.

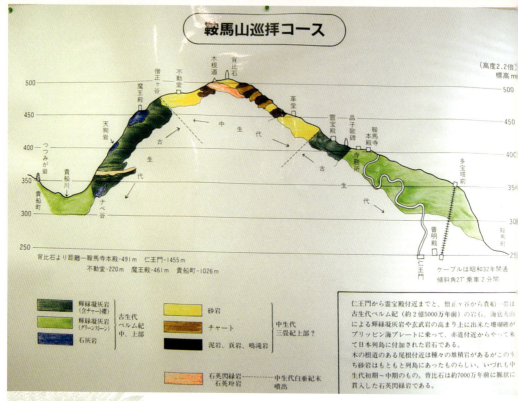

鞍馬山巡拝コース

Cross section of the mountain showing that areas near the bottom are older than the volcanic areas near the top.

A Tiger painting.

Diorama of the ancient sea life before Kurama Mountain rose.

104

There is an incredible variety of butterflies found on Kurama Mountain.

Ferns found on Kurama Mountain.

SECOND FLOOR: TEMPLE HISTORY

THE SECOND FLOOR HAS A HALLWAY, the historical exhibit room, and the memorial room for the poets Akiko and Tekkan Yosano.

HALLWAY

The hallway contains items from some past festivals. Of special note are the night photographs of the mountain. One in particular has a great towering tree. This tree is the famous Ōsugi Gongen, considered an incarnation of the god Maõ-son. The tree fell in a typhoon in 1950.

HISTORICAL EXHIBIT ROOM

The Historical Exhibit Room contains calligraphy, a short description of some of the festivals and picture scrolls. There are also various artifacts from the temple's past, small statues, a stone purification basin and items less easily identified. Of special interest is a picture scroll of the mountain. The first assumption

tion is that it is depicting the three deities of Kurama: Maõ-son, Bishamonten, and Kannon. Bishamonten is twice as large as the other two. The Kurama Tengu holds a fan. My translator said it was made between 1650-1700 A.D., and actually depicts Bishamonten with two supporting deities, and the larger tengu-like being with the fan is Maõ-son. Millipedes were considered to be messengers or servants of Bishamonten. Therefore, millipedes appear in a number of temple documents and artifacts in this room.

This ancient scroll shows Maõ-son (top right) and Bishmonten with his two attendants.

Yosano Memorial Room

Akiko Yosano (1868-1942) and her husband Tekkan were famous Japanese poets, famous for flouting social conventions, supporting women's rights, and protesting war. Calligraphy of a number of their poems is on display, as are some of their art, furniture, and clothing. The high priestess of Kurama Temple was a long-time supporter of the Yosanos. There are pictures of the Yosanos' visits to Kurama Temple on the walls of this room.

The Goddess Kannon with two attendants.

Poetry Screen.

THIRD FLOOR: STATUES

IN THE HALLWAY OF THE THIRD FLOOR is a statue of a tiger. To those of us who have seen tigers on TV, movies and in zoos, it does not look like a tiger. But the artist who sculpted this had never seen tigers, and had to do his best guessing what a tiger would look like, based on written descriptions and skins. The tiger was a very exotic and magical creature to the Japanese. It is almost mythical, like the dragon, because tigers are not native to Japan. It is an important animal in the zodiac and associated with the direction of South. Tigers are especially important to the Kurama Temple, because of Gantei's vision that led to the founding of the temple in the Year, Month, Day and Hour of the Tiger.

Visitors must remove their shoes before entering the statue room. This room is full of ancient statues, mostly of Bishamonten, with two of Kannon. Maõ-son is represented by wood from the sacred tree, Õsugi Gongen, which was considered a reincarnation of him. As one enters the statue room, there is a small seating area. There are notebooks here. One is

Statues of Maõ-son, Bishamonten and Kannon.

encouraged to write down a few thoughts about this room and
prayers to the deities within.

The statues in this room are Buddhist images from the Late
Heian (794-1185 A.D.) and Kamakura (1200-1300 A.D.) periods. Some are designated important cultural properties and one is
considered a national treasure. One of the Kamakura-era figures
is noted for carrying a sankozuka-no-ken, a sword with a blade at
one end and three prongs on the other. The prongs were originally
used to clear wild plants from the path by hermits and priests, but
they later came to symbolize chasing away devils.

Bishamonten.

Tiger carved by an artist who had never seen one.

WILDERNESS GATE

CLIMBING UP THE MOUNTAIN, the visitor passes through one last gate. This gate symbolizes the official entry into the wild part of the mountain. The sign on the gate asks the visitor to respect Kurama's status as a nature preserve. "Do not remove any animals, plants or minerals from the mountain. Be careful with fire. Carry your trash with you." -sign translation Visitors arriving at this point late in the day may go a little further, but should not attempt to hike all the way to Kibune, as the path from this point is unlit, less traveled and more rough. The main temple complex is about two-thirds the distance to the top of the mountain, but is only about one-third of the hiking distance to Kibune.

JIZŌ SHRINE

Kurama is not a tall mountain, but it is steep enough to encourage many visitors to pause and take a breath. This Jizō Shrine is just after one of the steeper parts on the mountain. Just before the shrine is a spring and purification shrine called Ikitsugi- no Mizu, which translates as Water to Breathe. Yoshitsune would drink from this spring after doing hard

training. Jizō is one of the most beloved of the Bodhisattvas of Japan. Like many of the Buddhist deities, Jizō is multilayered. He is considered, in his simplest form, as the protector of children, pregnant women, travelers and firemen. Jizō's mission is actually more profoundly to rescue souls caught in hell, both in this world and beyond.

One will notice on the altar cloths which adorn this temple, the original clock-

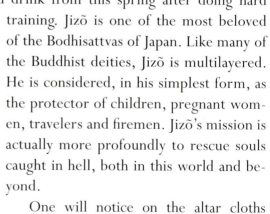

Inside the Jizō Shrine.

wise version of the swastika or Man-ji. This symbol has represented the creative forces of the universe in Buddhism for millennia. Although originally a Buddhist symbol, the Nazis used the counter-clockwise version to represent their beliefs in destruction.

Ki Note

The greatest power areas of Kurama Mountain are in the areas between the Jizō Shrine near the top of the mountain and Okunoin. The sites up to this point act as an introduction to the mountain and are the places most people visit. Few visitors continue past the main temple, and even fewer past the Kurama Museum and wilderness gate. Kurama has never been about buildings, but is about the power of these sacred places.

ECOLOGY NOTE: Erosion is an ongoing concern on Kurama Mountain. Rain and the steady stream of pilgrims, over the centuries, have had a strong effect on the mountain. The paths are being steadily upgraded from walking on the dirt, to walking on stairs and steps. Near the Jizō Shrine, the effect of centuries of erosion can be easily seen in the steep slopes.

This gateway leads to the wild half of the mountain.

平成十五年八月吉日

MEASURING STONE

A FTER SOME STEADY CLIMBING, the trail comes to the Measuring Stone with a small shrine beside it. This is the highest elevation on the mountain's main trail. The Japanese hero Yoshitsune measured his height against this stone when he was sixteen, before heading north to seek revenge for the deaths of his father and most of his clan. The measuring stone is enclosed by a small fence, and seems much too short to measure a sixteen year-old boy.

CEDAR TREES AT THE SUMMIT

The measuring stone is the landmark for where the path diverges. While most visitors continue straight down the trail at this point, taking a left here leads through a high energy stand of cedars, and then on to Ōsugi Gongen. The trail from Ōsugi Gongen rejoins the main path a little further down. Just off the main path, there are cedar roots. These cedar trees are especially high in natural energy because of their position on the peak of the mountain. The soil has eroded from around the roots to create a unique sight - a favorite for photographers. Legend has it that Yoshitsune practiced jumping among roots to improve his ability to keep his footing when fighting on uneven terrain.

Close-up of the measuring stone.

The Jizō Shrine.

The samurai hero, Yoshitsune, measured himself here before leaving Kurama.

Exposed cedar roots highlight Kurama's soil erosion.

Ki Note

TREE ENERGY EXERCISE: The trees here have an extraordinary energy. Some visitors like to stand between the tree trunks with their hands reaching out to the trunks on either side. Others like to place a hand between the root and the earth to feel the energy of the root pass over the palm.

Visitors touch the cedar trees at the summit on Kurama.

Cedar trees at the summit of Kurama Mountain.

Ōsugi Gongen

I F THE VISITOR CONTINUES THROUGH the cedars and beautiful trees, to the left away from the main trail, they can follow the path that leads to Ōsugi Gongen. This area has a small temple building, a group of rough wooden benches, and great trees. This is the best place on Kurama for peaceful contemplation because it is off the main path, and those wishing to sit quietly will not be disturbed. The visitor is invited to spend at least 20-30 minutes at this site in contemplation. Take the time to listen to the sounds of nature and to feel the place. Let your mind quiet itself, just be, and let the wisdom and power of the mountain speak to you. In one of the booklets of the temple, it refers to Ōsugi Gongen as a "meditation training place" and asks visitors to "Please sit on the benches and listen to the sounds of nature and be calm, listening to the inside of your heart."

A huge tree stood at this spot for well over a thousand years, until September of 1950 when it was knocked over by Typhoon Jane.[6] The remains of its trunk are visible behind the shrine. The tree was considered to be a reincarnation of the

The trees near the meditation site of Ōsugi Gongen are quite large.

God Maõ-son, the power of Earth. The tree rivaled in size the trees at the Yuki shrine, measuring at least eight feet across. The tree is mentioned in the entry for Kurama in a Kyoto guidebook from 1895[7]. The wood from part of Õsugi Gongen that fell was carefully taken away, and has been used for many of the temple's statues and sacred items. A piece of the tree even appears beside the more conventional statues of deities in the Kurama Museum.

There are benches in a rough semi-circle around the site. Now, most visitors sit facing outward towards the horizon (which can't really be seen because of the small trees). However, when the tree stood here, the natural direction to look was inward, towards the tree and its shrine. Many of the other trees still standing are most likely the offspring of the Õsugi Gongen tree.

To continue on to Kibune head downslope, to the right of where the Kurama village end of the trail entered the clearing. The trail soon rejoins the main trail. Kibune is still a substantial hike. Or turn around, and go back to where the trail came in, towards the main temple and the village of Kurama.

The Õsugi Gongen Temple.

This tree (Ōsugi Gongen) is considered to be an incarnation of the god Maō-son.

This marker is at the intersection back to the main trail.

Outside benches among the trees look northwest towards the horizon.

NOTES

REIKI HISTORY NOTES: For Reiki practitioners, this site holds special significance for it was most likely the spot where the founder of Reiki meditated for twenty-one days and received the Reiki energy.

REIKI ENERGY NOTES: The energy at Ōsugi Gongen is surprising; it is not an overpowering surge of ki. It is not a place that shouts its power. It is not even a place that makes the Reiki in your hands seem especially strong. It is more of a slow steady tide that builds, the longer you are there. The effects of meditating in this place are not fully realized until heading into lower energy environments, off the mountain.

Every time I am here long enough to spend some time, I get an incredible sense of the ordinary. Looking down at the dirt, the bark of the trees, and the benches here, there is a sense of precious reality to this place. While the surface of the mind may still chatter, the back of the mind becomes oddly quiet. My intuition has told me that it does not matter what I do here, whether I meditate, walk, eat lunch, or even read a book, it only matters that I come and take the time to do so. It is easy to spend time doing little here. While I would normally seek a book, conversation, or something to occupy my mind, while here on Ōsugi Gongen that seems less important.

When on Kurama I also notice the energy in my hands much less than usual. Much of how the human body processes sensation is by contrast to the sensation in the area around it. The energy on the mountain does not seem overwhelming or powerful because of how it raises the background level of energy around the practitioner.

It is when leaving the mountain that the effects of having spent time here become much more noticeable. The ordinary world seems less powerful; the energy in one's hands seems different. Many people also feel a sense of 'whelm,' not being overwhelmed by the energy present, but having as much as one can handle right now, and not wanting any more.

A hallmark of high-energy places is the effect that they have on the long-living things, namely trees. Trees concentrate the energy of an area. This energy often leads to unusual growth patterns in the trees. Spending some time looking around at the trees near the Ōsugi Gongen site reveals a number of unusual trees with oddly twisting branches, trees growing together, and unusual root formations.

Kurama Crest.

The path to Kibune is to the right of the path where the visitor arrived from Kurama Temple, on the down-hill side of the site. On the way to the main trail are several trees that were knocked down by a typhoon in the fall of 2004. The path soon rejoins the main trail, and the visitor should continue down the mountain.

Sword Boulder

On the trail between the summit of Kurama Mountain and the next major site of the Fudō Temple is an odd shaped boulder to the right of the trail. From some angles, the rock looks like a face. There are many lines crisscrossing the surfaces of the rock. Legend says that these lines are the sword cuts from when the samurai hero Yoshitsune practiced his swordsmanship.

Fudō Temple

The trail from the top of Kurama to Kibune next passes through a small clearing. To the left is a temple building dedicated to Fudō. (Not open to visitors). Embedded in the trail in front of the Fudō temple is a lotus mandala. Hidden inside the temple is a statue to Fudō that was made by Dengyo Daishi, also called Saicho who founded the Enryaku temple on Hiei Mountain. For much of its history, Kurama was a sub-temple of the Enryaku Tendai Temple. Fudō is the god who sits in the flames of life. He has long been the god of warriors who must stand in the adversity of battle. Spiritually, he symbolizes the one who remains in the 'heat' of the world saying: "All this is fuel for my enlightenment."

Fudō Temple.

MEDITATING ON FUDŌ

The Lotus Mandala in front of the Fudō temple is an energetic power spot. Visitors can stand in the center of the Fudō mandala, and ask Fudō to burn, bind or slay that which hinders enlightenment. After standing on this spot for several minutes, many feel a palpable sense of energy coming up from the earth beneath their feet.

SHRINE TO YOSHITSUNE

Further into the clearing on the right is a small shrine dedicated to the famed Samurai Yoshitsune. A nearby sign describes the history of his clan and his historic deeds. Yoshitsune's spirit is said to have returned to Kurama after his death, and is enshrined and honored at this shrine. A sign describes this area as follows: This location is where, according to legend, young Yoshitsune learned military arts from the Tengu whose name was Priest Zosei, and his followers.

One visitor said this area was a military encampment of Kurama warrior monks who took the name for their band from the legendary Tengu. Its location is one of the few flat areas of Kurama. It also straddled the ancient trail passing from Kyoto to the north, allowing them to control the traffic that passed through. Officials from Kyoto concerned about criminals escaping the city to the north would notify the warriors here to keep watch for them.

Yoshitune used to practice swordship among the roots on this path.

The Fudō Mandala.

The soul of the famous samurai hero Yoshitsune is enshrined here.

OKUNOIN MAÕ-DEN: THE INNER TEMPLE

THE LAST MAJOR SITE ON KURAMA IS OKUNOIN, the Inner Temple. There is a temple building with benches inside; an inner shrine, and a small plaza with benches. The inner shrine rests on a pile of rocks that are energetically very powerful. Geologically, the rocks are seabed limestone and fossilized coral. They were thrown into the air creating a volcano, that later became Mt. Kurama.

Temple documents describe an early vision of how Maõ-son landed at Okunoin, 6.5 million years ago. Maõ-son came to help with the evolution of the earth and mankind's conquest over wickedness. Maõ-son is considered to be 'the conqueror' of evil. A sign beside the stone garden describes the energy of this place:

"This is the place where the spirit can fly down to earth to help people and create world peace. When we humans can listen to the sounds of nature from a place of inner calm, then the greatness of nature can talk to us about the ways of the universe. In this holy place, many who have come before us have received answers to the reality of the self by listening to the ways of the universe. Protected by the deep green trees, they can connect to the mysterious world that has existed here for millions of years."

While many Reiki practitioners focus on Õsugi Gongen as the most powerful point on the mountain, others regard the summit of the mountain as the most powerful. For the people of Kurama temple, the Okunoin is the greatest power spot on the mountain.

There is a Japanese tradition of folding 1000 paper cranes as a form of prayer, usually for health. These cranes are left as offerings to the gods at temples.

Sword marks in the rock.

Kı Note

THE WIND OF SPIRIT: One of my Japanese friends has spoken to me, telling me that for herself, the presence of the breeze or wind is an indication of spirit, and the blessing of spirit. The feature of Okunoin that most amazes her is that every time she has been there, no matter how still the air elsewhere, a breeze is always blowing there, and always flows from the direction of the boulders towards the shrine.

POWER SPOTS AT OKUNOIN: There are many small power spots in this area. There are a number of rocks near the fenced in area that have very powerful energy, some inside the worship building, some outside. Standing on these rocks the energy can be felt pushing up into the feet. There are also several stumps in the area where trees once stood. The energy of the area is strong enough that if someone scans the area above the stump, the energy of the tree that stood there can still be felt.

The sacred rocks behind Okunoin are said to be where Maõ-son came to earth 6.5 million years ago.

Inner Temple of the Okunoin.

Unusual Trees

THE TRAIL CONTINUES DOWN FROM OKUNOIN towards the village of Kibune. While there are no more major sites on the trail there are many trees with unusual growth patterns, often next to the trail. Trees tend to be especially affected by living in high-energy areas because they live such long lives. Most of these trees occur in pairs, often growing together, showing twisted limbs or having other unusual growth patterns. Energy-aware visitors are likely to notice that the highest energy tends to cluster around these great trees.

Lovers' Tree

The two entwined trees that have grown together are called the Lovers' tree. Small offerings are often left at the shrine located at the base of the trees (not shown).

Opening between Worlds

This tree originally had two separate branches that grew together to create this small opening. The light shining through suggests an opening to a magical world.

Twisted Tree Vine This is the most spectacular of all of the oddly growing trees on the mountain. An enormous 'tree' grows mostly parallel to the path before its branches rise to intermingle with the leaves of the trees above. The tree appears to be a centuries-old kind of vine, which climbs the trunks of other trees to reach the sunlight. The people at the Kurama museum told us it is actually an ancient wisteria vine.

Lovers' Tree: a small shrine sits at its base.

Ki Note

The energy on this section of the trail is markedly different from elsewhere. There is a sharp slope between the more worldly 'normal energy' of Kibune village below and the energy of the mountain. Most visitors hurry quickly down or up this slope because they are either tired from climbing Kurama Mountain, or they are anticipating how much more they have to climb. The energy spots in this area seem exceptionally appreciative of visitors taking the time to connect to them.

Two twisting branches growing together.

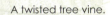

A twisted tree vine.

NISHIMON (WESTERN GATE) AND KIBUNE VILLAGE

THE TRAIL CONTINUES DOWN AND ENDS at the road through the village of Kibune. Just before the end, there is a small kiosk where visitors entering the mountain from this side can pay their entry fee to the temple (200 Yen). The trail then crosses the small, clear Kurama River at a bridge. Upon reaching the road, visitors can turn right (uphill) to go to the Kibune shrine, or turn left (downhill) to head towards the Kibune train station

Most of the buildings in Kibune village are restaurants, coffee shops, or Ryokans (traditional Japanese Inns). All are expensive ($40-$100 USD per person just for lunch), but pleasant. The coffee shops are in the $4-$6 USD per cup range, and can be a welcome place to sit after a long hike. English is not typically spoken, and menus are not found in English. For centuries Kibune has been famous for outdoor dining in the summer. A number of the restaurants have built dining-platforms directly over the river. The river-cooled air must have felt extraordinarily good in the days before electric fans and air conditioning.

Visitors who wish to go to the Kibune train station, to return to Kyoto, should go left. It is a twenty-five minute brisk walk from the Kurama Bridge. There is usually a bus waiting in a parking lot a quarter mile down the road from the bridge. This takes the visitors to the station in time for the next train. The cost of the bus is 220 yen (about $2 USD) and it is paid when getting off.

Kibune Shrine is described elsewhere. The walk from Kibune village to the Train Station is described on the following pages.

A small shelter with a thatched roof.

Small Jizō Shrine at the western entrance to Kurama.

REIKI NOTE

HISTORY: In both the Japanese and Western versions of the 'Reiki Story,' Mikao Usui meditated on the top of the mountain for twenty-one days. In Mrs. Takata's version of the story, after he had the experience, he ran down the mountain, stubbed his toe, and later found somewhere to have breakfast. If this experience occurred on top of Kurama Mountain, the most likely breakfast place was either Kurama village, on one side of the mountain, or Kibune village on this side.

The main street of Kibune is lined with restaurants, shops and Ryokan lodging.

This bridge is the Kibune exit from Kurama Temple.

KIBUNE SHRINE

CONTINUING UP THE ROAD FROM THE KURAMA BRIDGE (not down towards the Kibune Train Station) the Kibune Shrine will come into view. The Kibune Shrine is spread over two sites. The first site has the Oratory and main building of the shrine. The second site, farther up the road, is the original shrine. While the exact age of the Kibune Shrine is unknown, the original shrine structure was built around 400 A.D. The Kibune Shrine is actually centuries older than the Kurama Temple. The original (and now secondary) shrine began long ago when a female water Kami (spirit/god) came down from the sky in a boat, and found a spring there. This Kami's name is Okami-no-Kami. She is prayed to as a provider of water to others, in the form of ground springs, rain and snow. A shrine was built on Okami-no-Kami's original stone boat, by covering the boat with stones. A spirit rope placed around the shrine affirms its sacred nature.

The stone 'boat' where the kami of the shrine descended from the sky.

Entryway to Kibune Shrine.

The Kibune Shrine is famous for its water. Kibune is considered to be the symbolic source of water for Kyoto, and the water from its springs is considered pure and delicious. Visitors often bring containers to take it home for offerings to the spirits or for making tea. The current shrine was built around 1055 A.D. Many (unspecified) disasters damaged the original shrine. The long, lantern-lined stairway up to the shrine is a lovely feature. The statues of the horses at the main shrine commemorate their use as offerings to the shrine to improve the weather. A white horse was offered as an offering for fine weather, and a black horse was an offering for rain.

After Kyoto became Japan's capital in 794 A.D., the Imperial court worshipped at the Kibune Shrine as one of the twenty-two most special shrines in Japan. Offerings of horses were sent to the shrine to assure good weather for the region. There is also a famous Noh play called *Kanawa* where a jealous women goes to the Kibune Shrine and asks to be changed into a demon so she can get revenge.

Oratory.

Horse statues at Kibune Shrine.

Road to Kibune Station

I T IS ABOUT A TWENTY-FIVE MINUTE WALK from the Kurama Bridge in Kibune to Kibune train station. About five minutes south of the Kurama Bridge is the parking lot where the bus leaves for Kibune station. Others may opt to walk to the station. The Kurama River parallels the road. This mountain stream is known for its clear, rushing water. Bird watchers should look out for the Brown Dipper. This dark brown bird is about the size and shape of a robin, and actually walks under the water to forage for food.

Fire Fly Rock

On the road from Kibune, shortly before the station, some boulders have a red fence, these are called the Firefly Rocks. It was at this spot that the famed, romantic, poetess Izumi Shibuku (974-1033 A.D.) was inspired to write a poem.

When, after being forsaken by a man,
I made a pilgrimage to the Kibune shrine,
And at the Mitarashi River
[where it was hoped one could be purified of love yearning]
I saw the fireflies flying.

Kibune Station

The stairs to Kibune station are on the right-hand side of the road. This is the stop on the Eizan line just south of Kurama. Visitors should take the train south (right) to return to Kyoto. The shop below the station has a number of local souvenirs for sale. The bus to and from Kibune is timed to coincide with the arrival and departure of the trains, allowing the visitors a few minutes to browse inside.

In November, the fall foliage behind the train tracks is lit up.

Kibune Station.

A lovely stream runs alongside the road.

Fire Fly Rock inspired a famous Japanese poem.

KURAMA ONSEN

A GREAT WAY TO END THE DAY IS AT Kurama Onsen. (Onsen means hot spring.) An Onsen is a slightly fancier version of the Japanese public bath. Many of the visitors to Kurama village come soley for the purpose of going to the Kurama Onsen. It is one of the nicest outdoor hot springs in the area. For those who appreciate the energetic ki of the area, standing in the hot water pool of the Onsen is an amazing way to allow one's bare skin to fully connect to the energy of the mountain above.

The Onsen is reached from Kurama village. If one has climbed over the mountain to Kibune and wants to go to the Onsen, take the train one-stop to Kurama village. A free Onsen van meets most of the trains. If there is no van waiting at the train station, the Onsen is about a twenty-minute walk on the main road of Kurama. Go in the same direction as if going to the temple, but instead of climbing the stairs to the temple; continue along the main road until the Onsen is reached. Visitors who have never been to a Japanese bath or Onsen are recommended to bring someone of the same gender who has been to one before. This person can explain or demonstrate what is expected which is mainly to wash well before entering. Most importantly for modest visitors,

the bather should be comfortable being nude in front of strangers of the same gender: bathing suits are not allowed.

When entering from the parking lot, the main building is to the left. It contains a restaurant, a small souvenir sales area, vending machines and a Japanese Ryokan. The Ryokan lodging cost including an elaborate breakfast and dinner is about 17,000 yen or $170 per guest/per night with a recommended 2-3 persons to a room.

The smaller building straight ahead is the outdoor Onsen. Tickets for the outdoor Onsen and towels are available at a vending machine outside the Onsen building, i.e. straight ahead. The Onsen costs about 1200 yen/$12, with a souvenir towel costing an extra 200 yen ($2.00). Upon entering the building, visitors take off their shoes and put them in the alcove. The visitors then enters the men's or women's main changing room and remove all of their clothes and put them into a locker.

The next room contains the showers. The visitor then goes into the shower area, rinses off a stool and sits down in front of a shower spigot. Wash very thoroughly with the soap and shampoo provided before going outside into the walled bath area. Most people are pretty quiet in the baths; please follow suit and if you are going to talk to a friend, speak quietly. Soak as long as you wish, and gaze upon the mountain above. Energetically many experience a strong sense of communion with the mountain, and absorb its energy into every cell of the body.

PRACTICAL
GUIDE

A Guide for Foreign Travelers

Introduction:

This guide is intended for those brave souls who are planning to go to Kurama Mountain on their own. It covers issues that will concern non-Japanese visitors in Japan for the first time. It is for those not familiar with Japanese customs who are planning a visit to the mountain. It covers very basic information about bathrooms and restaurants, etiquette when visiting a shrine, and information on what to bring on a trip to Kurama. Basic tips on how to read train schedules will also be covered. This guide is not intended to replace a travel guide to Japan, or your own searches on the web. Ordinary people should be able to do extraordinary things, including going on a trip to Japan. A trip to Japan does not have to be expensive, but it does have some challenges.

Travel Advice

How to Get to Kyoto

The best way to get to Kyoto is to fly into Kansai International Airport in Osaka (KIX). Check around carefully on airfares. Typically Japanese travel agents can get you a better fare. Many are available through the Internet. Round trip tickets from Los Angeles are between $500-$700 round trip off season, including tax. Also make a reservation for MK Taxi to pick you up at the airport and bring you directly to the hotel. The journey is just under three hours. (People do not typically tip taxis in Japan.) MK Taxi Skyshuttle costs 3000 yen (about $30) including 1 large bag or suitcase. There is a charge of 1000 yen for each additional large bag. They will ask you how many large bags you will have when you make the reservation. MK Taxi has an English language web site: www.mk-group.co.jp/english/html.htm

Where to Stay in Kyoto

While there are Japanese-style Ryokan Inns in Kurama and Kibune, they are very expensive. They cost about $175 plus, per person, per night, with a three-person minimum per room. This includes an elaborate Japanese-style breakfast and dinner, with Japanese-style sleeping on a futon, on the floor.

It is more inexpensive to stay in Kyoto city for one-half of the cost of a Kurama/Kibune Ryokan and take the twenty-five minute train ride to the mountain from Demachiyanagi Station. There are many places in Kyoto to stay. The city has an excellent bus, subway and taxi system. Hostel-style accommodations can be found for about $30/night. Reasonable hotels can cost well under $100/night. (There are a number of $300/night places as well.) If Kurama is the major reason for being in Kyoto, select an accommodation near the Eizan Line, in the Northeast quadrant of the city. Kyoto has an incredible number and variety of things to see and do, so be sure to leave enough time to explore.

BRINGING YEN

Get at least several hundred dollars of Yen currency before leaving for Japan, either at the airport or from your local bank. The exchange rate is roughly 100 yen to the dollar, which simplifies calculating costs in Japan. Just move over two decimal places, so 3,000 yen becomes about $30. (As of this writing the exchange is actually closer to 115 to the dollar.) Most major hotels will exchange currency for their guests. Most smaller hotels do not. There are plenty of places in Kyoto to exchange currency, but they are all located in the business districts. If you are staying outside the center of town, or in the villages of Kurama or Kibune, it is inconvenient to get currency. Credit cards are far less universally accepted in Japan, and Visa is often the only one accepted. Verify whether your lodging accepts credit cards before going to Japan. Japan is full of ATMs, however, very few of them will accept foreign ATM cards. As of 2006, the ATMs in many Japanese Post Offices allow foreign visitors to use their cards to make withdrawals. There are plans for more ATMs in the future to allow foreign bank withdrawals.

NOTE: Bring a photocopy of your passport, emergency contact information, drug prescriptions, drug allergies, or any other information that might be important in case of trouble. Also include where you are staying in Japan. Keep one copy in your luggage, one copy with you, and give copies to the people traveling with you.

Don't go Kurama Mountain if...

THIS TRIP IS NOT FOR EVERYONE. There are a number of people I highly recommend should not go on this trip.

Don't go if you can't hike!

Kurama is not handicap accessible. There are numerous stairs and climbing involved that can't be avoided. Visitors should be in good shape. Kurama is a mountain. If you are not athletic, or if you only do athletics in a gym, it is highly recommended that you do some mountain or hill-hiking to prepare yourself for the trip. Hiking on flat land or using a treadmill uses a different set of muscles than mountain hiking. If you don't have mountains in your area, consider stair climbing, up and down in an apartment or office building.

Visitors in only fair shape, but still able to do some hiking can take the cable car to below the Main Temple complex. They will miss some of the sites on the mountain including the Ōsugi Gongen tree where Mikao Usui meditated for twenty-one days; but at least they will have some time on the mountain. Additionally, less limber visitors may have another difficulty. Some places have western toilets; some do not, and require squatting. (See restrooms)

Don't go if you are on a special diet

On the whole, Japanese restaurant food is much healthier than American restaurant food, with smaller and thus lower calorie portions. Japanese food is varied and interesting and exploring the culture through its food is an important feature of any trip, especially if you can meet up with some locals. However, especially for the casual traveler unfamiliar with the area, Japan is not special diet friendly. The diet is, almost universally, 60% refined starch, either white rice or noodles, 25% meat or fish, and 15% vegetable, and high in salt (usually in the form of soy sauce or miso). Special orders, even if you speak Japanese, are generally just not done. Bread is always white.

Vegetarian restaurants exist, but not really enough to sustain vegetarians for an entire trip. Brown rice is not usually available. Vegetables, including salads, are considered a flavoring for the rice, and not proportionally large enough to be a meal. I know of no "Soup and Salad" restaurants in Kyoto, though some 'family restaurants' do have a meal sized salad. Soup broth may have a fish, pork, mushroom or kelp base. Vegetables are well cooked. Organic food is rare but increasingly popular in certain specialty stores. Visitors needing a lot of vegetables or raw foods will want to supplement their diet from grocery stores.

Japan is even more difficult for those on a low carbohydrate diet. Most meat and fish dishes consist of a small amount of meat served with a large amount of starch. Japan is also hard if you don't like Japanese food, There are a few steak places, but they tend to be expensive, as some Chinese food places. For those needing a dose of the familiar (regardless of its health value) there are even McDonalds, Kentucky Fried Chicken, Mister Donut and Starbucks. Convenience stores and grocery stores can be a useful way to supplement your diet. In addition to getting fresh fruit, they also have prepared foods that you can take back to your hotel. Department stores also tend to have an entire floor, typically the basement, dedicated to prepared foodstuffs; it is worthwhile to go just to see the huge variety there. Those with food allergies will also have to be careful, because unless you speak Japanese, you cannot ask what is/isn't in a food. You may wish to have a Japanese speaking friend write something down for you about any special allergies so you can show the waiter. There is more on eating in Japan in the restaurant section that soon follows.

DON'T GO IF YOU ARE AN IMPATIENT OR FUSSY TRAVELER

Traveling is always a risky enterprise. There are always things that are far better than the visitor expected, and things that are not as good. A good traveler can handle this with grace. Traveling to a foreign country, where everyone speaks and reads a language that you don't, requires patience to figure things out on your own, and a sense of humor is helpful for things that can't be handled. Don't expect that people will speak in English. While most Japanese learn English in school, they do not typically use it afterwards. Most are far better at reading English than speaking or understanding it. Writing out what you are looking for may get you better results. Most are also shy about what they know, and often speak more English than they let on at first.

Japan is a very modern country with sanitation and facilities as up to date if not more so as anywhere in the United States. But the traveler not accustomed to traveling outside the United States may still have some trouble adjusting to differences in custom. Do your best to fit in, and realize the people you are interacting with have in all likelihood dealt with people like you before.

RESTAURANTS

HOW DOES ONE ORDER FOOD IN A COUNTRY where one can't read or speak the language? Very few places will have English menus. A name in English on the sign is no guarantee that English is spoken inside. One quickly learns to appreciate plastic display food. Outside, many restaurants will have plastic models of the food they serve inside. If needed, take the waiter outside and point to what you want. The word for water is mizu (Me-zoo). Do not try to eat at a restaurant that does not post its prices, unless you have someone with you who knows the restaurant. Meals can be very expensive in some places; $100/person is not uncommon. However, most restaurants are more reasonable, just slightly higher than in a major U.S. city. Bakeries are one of the truly unexpected joys of being in Japan. Kyoto has many bakeries with fresh baked croissants, rolls and other baked treats. Coffee is another oddity in Japan. Coffee (called Ko-hee) can be found in vending machines (usually sweetened). There are many coffee shops: Japanese chains, local places and even Starbucks. They even serve coffee in fast food places. Depending on WHERE you buy coffee it can cost about the same as it does in the U.S., or truly gourmet coffee for about $5 to $8 a cup with no refills. Pay attention to where you go and enjoy what you find. For those who are less health conscious, fast food can be an economical way of getting underway quickly. There are both Japanese and Western fast food chains.

It is highly recommended to visit the basement food department of at least one department store to see the international variety of foods available. Kurama and Kibune villages do not have fast food or convenience stores. They do have some noodle places. Restaurants in Kibune are more expensive. Visitors to Kurama or even sightseeing in Kyoto might plan on keeping some snack food and drinks with them in case they can't find somewhere suitable to eat. Many visitors picnic on Kurama, bringing food with them. Three foods frequently found in Japan are tofu, pickled vegetables and seaweed. They are found everywhere, including soups and side dishes. Waiters are not tipped in Japan. The visitor not familiar with Japanese food, (or only familiar with Sushi and Tempura) might wish to eat in their local Japanese restaurants to familiarize themselves with the food before coming to Japan. There are also many great websites that describe and picture the different types of food.[8] Some of my Japanese favorites are Domburi, Tonkatsu and Oden, Enjoy!

Lunch of rice with chicken, cold dipping noodles, miso soup and pickles.

Far Left: Plastic food outside a restaurant.

Left: Tofu section in the supermarket.

RESTROOMS

JAPANESE RESTROOMS REQUIRE a great deal more explanation than they do in America. This discussion will include aspects of restrooms that the visitor will likely encounter in Japan, when hiking on Kurama Mountain, at restaurants or other shops, or when in private homes or hotels. Most parts of Japan are very civilized, however Kuramayama is a mountain wilderness, so on most of the mountain conditions are more primitive. Typically public restrooms are much cleaner and better kept than restrooms in similar places in the United States, but there are some cultural differences. Most Japanese public toilets have a solid door, so it is polite to knock on the door to see if someone is in there. Also, if someone knocks on the door, they are not trying to rush you, just discover if someone is inside. Just knock back to let them know you are in there.

Bring Toilet Paper with You

Traditionally, public restrooms do not have toilet paper or soap. Most places now will have these, but occasionally the visitor will find a place that does not, so it is helpful to keep a packet of tissues on hand and some hand sanitizer. In some of Kyoto's main shopping areas, people on the street will hand out packets of tissue with advertising on them. Paper towels are also not always found in restrooms, so it is useful to have a handkerchief with you.

Finding the Toilet

First of all, do not ask for the bathroom. Probably dating to an age back when septic plumbing was much less reliable, tradition placed the room with the bath in a different part of the house than the room with the toilet.[9] For public toilets, the universal male/female icon may be used; the room may be labeled "WC" for water closet, or it may be labeled in Japanese.(see picture) It is also common to have to go outside to reach the room where the toilet is.

TOILET SLIPPERS

If there is pair of slippers just inside the bathroom, take your shoes or house slippers off, leaving them outside the door, and put the toilet slippers on. Private homes and hotels will have toilet slippers, department stores and mountain facilities usually don't. Wear the toilet slippers while in the restroom, and then when leaving, put your own shoes or house slippers back on. If one forgets to use the toilet slippers, or leaves the toilet slippers on after leaving the toilet, it is considered impolite and unsanitary.

VARIETIES OF TOILETS

In America, toilets are pretty standard. In Japan, there is a much greater variety. The two basic types of flushing toilets are: the familiar western toilets, at which one sits down, and the Asian porcelain toilet nicknamed the 'squatter', because to use it, one squats facing the slightly raised hood. Urinals are also common. The Asian 'squatter' is considered to be more sanitary, as no part of the body touches the facility. The western style toilet is considered to be more comfortable for people who can't easily squat down.

Western-style toilets in Japan may also have a row of buttons on one side with 'features'. Most common are heated seats and bidets to rinse off one's lower anatomy. Another feature in some restrooms is the 'sound effect' buttons on the wall; often activated by just passing your hand over it. It is considered impolite to actually hear the sound of someone using the toilet, so some places have a button which makes running water sounds to cover over the sound! Most toilets have a simple flush lever. Occasionally there may either be a floor pedal or a button to push. Some toilets have a lever, which can be flushed in two directions, one for a big flush, and one for a little flush, allowing water to be conserved.

When hiking on Kurama Mountain, the facilities vary on different parts of the mountain. There are flushing, squatter toilets at the Kurama train station. There is a single western-style toilet in the ladies restroom across from the nursery school, and several flushing-squatters. Most of the other restrooms on the mountain are squatter style outhouses.

WASHING YOUR HANDS

In Japan, most of the restrooms will have a place to wash your hands. However, not all of them have a place to dry them. Visitors typically keep a handkerchief with them for doing so. In the mountain wilderness of Kurama, not all restrooms have soap, and the many remote sites do not have sinks, so hand sanitizer is useful.

Asian Style toilet. Squat facing the raised hood, flush by pushing button on the wall

TRAINS

IT SEEMS SO SIMPLE; just take the train from Demachiyanagi station to Kurama, however. there are a few things the visitor needs to know; such as how to buy a ticket, which train to get on, and how to read the train schedule. When getting on the train, be sure to be on the correct side of the tracks or you will be boarding the train and going in the wrong direction. In Japan, people drive on the left side of the road. Similarly, the trains go the same way. To go north to Karuma, face north on the tracks, and go to the station on the left (western) side of the track.

GETTING ON THE TRAIN

Getting on the right train is not difficult. Look at the front of the train for the name "Kurama." Kurama is the last station on the line, so this makes it simple. Demachiyanagi is the last station on the other end, making the return also simple. If the visitors' hotel is near a different station, just make a note of its name, and watch the signs at the station's train stops. There is also a sign in romanji (English letters) in every train car that shows the order of the stops.

BUYING A TICKET

The easiest way to pay for the buses, trains and subways in Kyoto is to buy a Kansai card, more formally called a Surutto Miyako Kansai card, which is available at major stations in various 1000 yen denominations from the same machine one can buy other tickets. Insert the card into the card reader machine when getting on. Then insert it again when leaving, and the system automatically calculates the fare and deducts it from the card. If the card runs out mid-transit, just go to the fare adjustment machine and pay the difference.

If you don't have a card, there are vending machines to buy exact cost tickets at both ends of the Eizan Line. They take a little patience to figure out. Cost is based on how many 'zones' you will cross through. There is a sign above that shows the zones. The zone the visitor is at is highlighted in red. Find the station to exit, and look in the box to pay the price. If you can't figure out the fare, the far simpler solution is to just buy the ticket on the train. Get on the train, and once the train is in motion, the conductor will come around and ask what stop you are getting out at; say 'Koo-ra-ma' and hand him the money. When in doubt, give him a 1000 yen bill, and let him give change. It will be less than 500 yen each way. If he wants to know anything else, it is probably the station the visitor got on. If necessary point to the start and end stations on the sign in the car. Hold onto the ticket to give it to the conductor when leaving the train.

How to Read the Train Schedule

First of all, don't panic if this is too confusing. Trains run at least twice an hour, from Demachiyanagi station to Kurama and back from 5:00 a.m. to 11:00 p.m. There are schedules at every train stop, and the trains for the most part do run on time. The schedule on the northbound side of the tracks (West Side) shows the northbound schedule, the schedule on the southbound side of the tracks (East Side), shows the southbound schedule.

The top left side of the sign tells what station one is at, followed by the end station of that direction. The first two kanji characters say Kurama Mountain, followed by the dot, followed by the kanji characters for Demachiyanagi station. The schedule consists of a blue panel that is the weekday schedule and a red schedule that is the weekend and holiday schedule. The numbers from 5 to 23 down the left side of the panel are the hours in a 24-hour period of time. 5:00 a.m. is 5, 12:00 p.m. is 12, 1:00 p.m. is 13 and 11:00p.m. is 23. The '10-15' line indicates the schedule is identical every hour between 10-15 (i.e. between 10:00 a.m. and 3:00 p.m.).

The numbers on each line are the minutes after the hour the train will arrive/depart at this station. For example, if you arrive at the station at 10am the sign tells you that the next few trails will be at 10: 03, 10:10, 10:18 and 10:21. However not all of these trains go to Kurama. The symbol above the minutes show the final destination for the train. Kurama is the last stop on the line. Therefore look for the Kanji for Kurama, which to me looks like 2 people standing together. The trains leaving for Kurama are at 10:03 and 10:18. Once the train arrives, double-check the train's final destination by looking at the sign on the front of the train, which will have the name of the train's final destination in roman letters.

鞍馬・八瀬 比叡山口方面　標

平日（月～金）[秋特別ダイヤ]

時	分
5	鞍27　八46　八57
6	鞍3　市13　八19　鞍23　八31　市34　八50　市54
7	八0　鞍3　修7　八10　市14　二18　鞍23　八27　修29　市34　八38　鞍43　八48　市55
8	鞍3　八5　二8　八12　市15　鞍23　八27　修29　市35　八40　鞍43　修46　八50　市55　八59
9	鞍3　市15　修17　八19　鞍23　二34　八39　鞍43　二50　八59
10	鞍3　八10　鞍18　八21　二30　鞍34　八39　鞍48　二54　八59
11	鞍3　八10　鞍18　八24　鞍27　八33　鞍40　鞍48　八54　二57
12	鞍3　八10　鞍18　八24　鞍27　八33　鞍40　鞍48　八54　二57
13	鞍3　八10　鞍18　八25　鞍33　八40　鞍48　八55
14	鞍3　八10　鞍18　八25　鞍33　八40　鞍48　八55
15	鞍3　八10　鞍18　八25　鞍32　八39　二42　鞍48　二54　八59
16	鞍3　二10　鞍18　八23　二30　八39　鞍43　八50　二55
17	八0　鞍3　八12　市15　鞍23　八28　市35　八40　鞍43　八50　市55
18	八0　鞍3　八13　市15　鞍23　八29　市35　八40　鞍43　八50　市55
19	八0　鞍3　八14　市17　修23　八30　鞍34　八41　市45　修55
20	八0　鞍5　市13　八15　八28　鞍34　八43　市45　八58
21	鞍3　八13　市15　八28　鞍34　市43　八45　八58
22	鞍4　市18　八20　八37　鞍40　市48　八57
23	鞍5　市17　八20　二38　修51　修57

備考
鞍…鞍馬行　　修…修学院行　　二…二軒茶屋行
八…八瀬 比叡山口行　　市…市原行

NATURAL HAZARDS OF
CLIMBING KURAMA MOUNTAIN

FIRST, KURAMA MOUNTAIN IS A VERY SAFE mountain to hike. It is less than 1000-feet of elevation to climb, so sneakers should be fine. There are some areas where there are eroded cedar roots protruding out of the earth, and the path near Kibune can be slippery in wet weather, but as long as the visitor is reasonably careful, it is unlikely to be a problem. Also, the path is clearly marked, and there is, except for the loop around Ōsugi Gongen, only one path, making it easy to not get lost. If you are planning to hike the whole mountain over to Kibune, then be sure to bring water and snacks with you, especially in hot weather. (See the 'what to bring list below.') Although quite rare, Kurama Mountain does have one species of poisonous snake, bears, and wild monkeys, which the average visitor is unlikely to encounter. There are Japanese signs warning of these wild animals. Be careful around rock piles and other sunny areas where snakes like to sun themselves. Do not poke your hand into, or move, around any stones in the quarried rock pile next to the Chumon Gate. Also, watch for snakes on the rock wall near the pathway from the upper cable car station to the Future Buddha Temple. Bears have been seen by some on the wilder parts of the mountain. Do not bother them, and definitely do not feed them. Wild monkeys love to grab glasses, purses, and other items; especially from children and petite people, so hold onto your things carefully if you see them.

How To Pray, Light
Incense and Candles

Shinto Purification

In front of each sacred Shinto site, you will see a purification shrine, known in Japanese as chozubachi. Shinto is a religion of purification and respect. Outside every sacred place where purification is recommended, there will be a purification shrine. Take the ladle, fill it with water and rinse your hands. Fill it again using water from the spout, and pour a little water into one hand. Put the water in your mouth to rinse it and spit it out into the gravel.

How to Pray

First, get the attention of the gods. If there is a bell, pull the rope and ring it twice. The bell is usually wooden or metal, and may clatter rather than ring when rung. If there is no bell, then clap twice. The first clap or ring is to attract the attention of sacred energies of heaven; the second is to attract the sacred energies of earth. Then bow to the shrine. In Japan the bow is performed with the eyes looking towards the ground, not towards the person or shrine one is bowing to. Then pray briefly. After praying bow again.

Photographing Sacred Objects

Many of the statues on Kurama Mountain have signs asking that no photographs be taken. This is largely an art preservation measure. Many of these statues are dimly lit, and require the use of a flash. The bright light of the flash can fade the paint, especially with the repetition of many people taking pictures of the same statue over the decades.

Don't Blow Out the Flame

The breath is considered impure in Japan, as are the fingers. The correct way to blow out the flame on lit incense is to wave it around in the air, or to use one's hand to wave the air over it.

Incense and Candles

Candles and incense are available for sale on Kurama Mountain. These items can be bought both at the Yuki shrine and at the Main Hall. The temple candles used on Kurama are hollow on the bottom, so they can be safely placed on the upright spikes. The main temple also sells pillar candles with the Heart Sutra written on them. Stick incense is also available for sale. There are two kinds. The green sticks are 'the cheap kind,' and are considered suitable for use anywhere on the mountain. The tan colored sticks are a bit more expensive and are considered 'the good kind.' Some people use these for offerings on the mountain, but most people buy this incense to bring home.

What to Bring for a Day on the Mountain

Day Pack

Good walking shoes. You will need to remove them at one location

Water bottle and water, snack food

Money (yen) for the train, entrance fee, lunch and souvenirs

Small plastic bag for trash

Tissues for toilet paper (not all bathrooms have it)

Hand sanitizer

Handkerchief (to dry your hands)

Camera and Film or Memory cards, Batteries

Temple candles (can also be purchased on mountain)

Matches or lighter (to light candles and incense)

Incense (can also be purchased on mountain)

Notebook and pen

Mosquito repellent (if spring/summer/early fall)

Appropriate sweater/rain gear — dress in layers

Clothing appropriate to the weather and for being outside all day

Postcards with Japanese postcard stamps (70 yen each to send abroad) and airmail stickers

Japanese phrase book

This Book!

EXPLAINING REIKI TO THE JAPANESE
(AND HOW NOT TO)

THE VERY WORD "REIKI" can be off-putting to the Japanese. While the word "Ki" simply means 'energy', the word 'Rei' is more problematic. The word 'Rei' is very similar to the English word 'spirit'. Depending on the context, the word 'spirit' in English, can mean spiritual, ghost or even alcohol. Similarly the Japanese word "Rei" can mean 'ghost/occult', 'cold' or 'spiritual.' While in English, the most common association with spirit has become 'spiritual,' but in Japan the most common association for "Rei" is 'ghost/occult.' The very idea of Rei Ki brings up ideas of supernatural beings throwing lightning bolts at each other. This is hardly the association most Reiki people had in mind!

Japan has three writing systems. Kanji are the familiar Chinese characters, where each character represents a word idea or part of a word. Hiragana and Katakana syllabaries are used to represent words as a series of sounds, and for particles and verb endings. The Vortex School in Tokyo does not use the Kanji for spelling the word Reiki, but the katakana lettering system, used for spelling foreign words.

Explaining Reiki to people in Japan is a challenge, especially if you don't speak Japanese! I have had some success with the following technique. I say, "Like Kikō" and make an energy ball in my hands, and turn my hands as if to Reiki myself. Kikō is the Japanese form of chi kung (also spelled chi gong). Kikō practitioners do energetic exercises to build their internal energy, then use the hands on the body or in the aura to transfer this energy to the client. More importantly, even among Japanese that have no idea what Kikō is, it is considered to be harmless, and probably beneficial. It is similar to the attitude many Americans have towards tai chi chuan. After this explanation, (and perhaps a demonstration) if I use the word Reiki, they have the correct definition of Rei in mind, and the word no longer seems so odd.

Japanese are skittish about anything that can be considered a cult in Japan. The Oum or Aum Shinrikyo sect is still feared because of their sarin nerve gas attack on the subways in 1995.

Making A Reiki Pilgrimage

As the place where Mikao Usui meditated and received Reiki, a visit to Kurama Mountain is a sacred pilgrimage.

Increase your Reiki Energy

Every time I go to Kurama I feel a significant and lasting increase in the amount of Reiki that flows through my hands. While intellectually I expected to be drawn to meditating solely at where Usui did, the reality has been that I have received great benefit from meditating at the many sites along the way, and asking the energy of Reiki to bless me at each. The average visitor can hike on Kurama Mountain without a problem, generally making the whole trip in half a day. Visitors wishing to make a pilgrimage will benefit from allowing more time, preferably in half-day increments.

Part of a pilgrimage is also the dealing with discomforts, crankiness, tiredness and overwhelms. Visitors should do their best not to be too hard on themselves in the process. The energy of the experience will most likely come upon the visitors when they are least aware. If one is pushing to experience everything, one will experience nothing. The greatest asset a spiritual pilgrim has is time. Come and spend time. Even if that means not seeing everything, it is better to fully take in the energy of what you see. Notice things. Some of the most powerful places on the mountain are NOT where you expect. The energies of the mountain will talk to you when and where they please. A pilgrimage to a sacred site is a combination of opening oneself to the sacred energies as fully as possible, and trying to stay grounded enough between times to function.

I recommend bringing a camera for taking a few photos of oneself on Kurama, and then putting it away. If people want to see pictures, show them this book. Picture taking has a way of distancing the person from the experience in the moment. I achieved far less spiritually on the mountain on the days when I focused on the camera, but I felt it was a necessary sacrifice to bring this book into being. Light candles and incense. Light one for the world, one for Reiki, and one for your own development and enlightenment.

GROUNDING

The energy of Kurama is very high. It does not always strike visitors as such when they first arrive, but prolonged exposure can leave the spiritually awake person feeling spacey and cranky, especially on the natural second half of the mountain. Typically this occurs because the people have received more energy than they can comfortably handle, and the solution is to ground the extra energy into the earth. But when the energy of Kurama deeply connects to people, the ground has more energy than the people do, making grounding difficult. You cannot ground people on a star! Snack foods and water can help. Some get benefit by releasing energy upward or by leaning against trees. But the best solution is getting these people off the mountain as quickly as possible.

FASTING

Even though Mikao Usui is said to have fasted for twenty-one days, it is NOT recommended that visitors fast for even a single day, unless their bodies are well accustomed to being in high energy areas and doing physical activity while fasting.

DEITIES

There are numerous deities on Kurama Mountain. In this section, the different types of deities are introduced in order of importance, followed by descriptions of each deity in alphabetical order.

Types of Deities

Tendai Buddhist Deities

Many of the deities on Kurama have eleven centuries of association with Tendai Buddhism. Although Kurama Mountain is now associated with the Kurama Kōkyō sect, Tendai deities are still honored. The four types of Tendai Buddhist deities are described below. Their Japanese names appear in parenthesis.

Buddhas (Nyorai)

Buddhas are fully–realized divine beings. The historical Buddha is one. The word Buddha is not a personal name but a title of praise like "Messiah." There is a statue of the Amida Buddha in the Lotus Wheel Hall. Those who pray to Amida will be reborn into the Pure Land, a place of Enlightenment.

Bodhisattva (Bosatsu) (pronounced Bow-sah-tsu)

The second type of deity is the Bodhisattva, in Japan, the Bosatsu. The Bodhisattva is a being that has reached Enlightenment, but instead of passing into Nirvana, or Heaven, this being has chosen to help other beings reach the path to Enlightenment. Kannon, one of Kurama's main deities, is the Bodhisattva of Serene Compassion. There are numerous shrines dedicated to the Bodhisattva Jizō, who is a protector of children, firemen, travelers and lost souls. Kannon and Jizō are the two most popular Bodhisattvas in Japan.

Miroku Bosatsu (Sanskrit Maitreya) is currently a Bodhisattva, but will be the Buddha who will appear at the end of time. There is a temple to the Maitreya Buddha near the upper cable car station.

Kings of Light (Myo or Myo-o)

The third type of beings in Tendai Buddhism is called the

Myo (or myo-o) (pronounced Me-yo) "Kings of Light," or "Heavenly Kings." These fierce looking beings assist the Buddhas to vanquish evil and to help humans resist temptation. The Myo are considered to be less important than the Bodhisattvas, but more important than the Ten (Devas). Fudō Myo is the chief of the Myo, and has a temple on the mountain. He helps people to conquer their inner demons.

DEVAS (TEN)

The Ten (Sanskrit Devas) can also be found in Hinduism. However, in Buddhism these beings often aid the defenders of the faith. (While pronounced Ten, it has nothing to do with the number 10) Several of the Ten are considered important enough to be worthy of worship. These include Bishamonten and Benzaiten. One of Kurama's main deities is Bishamon, the Japanese version of the Hindu god Vishnu, actually known as Bishamonten, in Japanese. Another Ten who has a temple shrine is Benzaiten, or Benten, patroness of music and the arts. She is similar to and derived from the Hindu goddess Sarasvati. Additionally, the guardians of Kurama's entry gate, the Niō, are also considered to be Ten.

INCORPORATION OF LOCAL DEITIES AND LEGENDS

Tendai Buddhism allows the incorporation of local deities into the belief system of a particular temple. The local deity is considered to be a manifestation of a more traditional Buddhist deity. Maō-son is an important local deity. He is considered to be a manifestation of Vajrayaksa, a deity from India. Akai-go-henzenjin is a minor local deity. She is the spirit of the magical snake that guards the well near the main temple.

KURAMA-KŌKYŌ BUDDHIST DEITIES

Elevation of Sonten as a deity appears to be part of the Kurama-Kōkyō sect's contribution to the religious philosophy of the mountain. This sect took over the mountain in 1949. Ever since the architect of the Toji Temple had a vision in the year 790 of Kannon and Bishamonten springing from the same source, the concept of all three of Kurama's deities proceeding from the same source became a logical conclusion. Sonten is considered to be "All That Is," the guiding principle of God. He is considered to be the divine principle behind the entire cosmos. Sonten is considered to be the sum of the trinity of Kurama's major deities, Maõ-son, Kannon and Bishamonten.

JAPAN'S SEVEN LUCKY GODS

Three of Japan's Seven Lucky Gods are honored on Mt. Kurama. The three include Bishamonten, Benzaiten and Fukurokuju. The Seven Lucky Gods, (essentially the same as the Chinese Gods of Luck) are a popular motif in Japan. They are often portrayed sailing on a boat of treasure. The Japanese Seven Lucky Gods are Ebisu (fisherman, rice farmers, commerce), Daikokuten (wealth, flood control), Benzaiten (music fine arts, longevity), Hotei (contentment and happiness-Maitreya), Fukurokuju (wisdom and longevity), Jurojin (longevity) and Bishamonten (warriors, treasure).

SHINTO DEITIES: THE KAMI

The Shinto deities of Kurama, called kami, are different in character from Buddhist deities. They are not pictured as having a specific form, but considered to be more of a natural feature or area with a concentrated Ki energy. Anything that is considered excellent can be treated as a kami; a famous ancestor, a spring or even a sword. All of the purification shrines and many of the springs and extra-large trees on Kurama are also considered to be kami.

Yoshitsune's spirit is considered to be a kami, and is enshrined near the Fudō Temple. Fujiyama (Mt. Fuji) near

Tokyo, is also considered to be a kami. Sometimes kami have a 'spirit rope' hanging around them. This is a rope with tassels, made out of white paper, and shaped as lightening bolts. In some cases a small 'house' has been erected for the spirits. Buddhism and Shinto are intertwined to such a degree that some places on Kurama have both Buddhist and Shinto features. There is a Shinto purification shrine on either side of the Buddhist main temple complex. To enter the temple for the Maitreya Buddha, one walks through a Shinto *torii*.

The Yuki Shrine is the main Shinto location on Kurama. There are three kami trees, a sacred spring, and a building where they sell blessed items and other shrine souvenirs. The Shinto Oratory was moved from the Imperial Palace in the year 940 A.D. to help spiritually protect the capital.

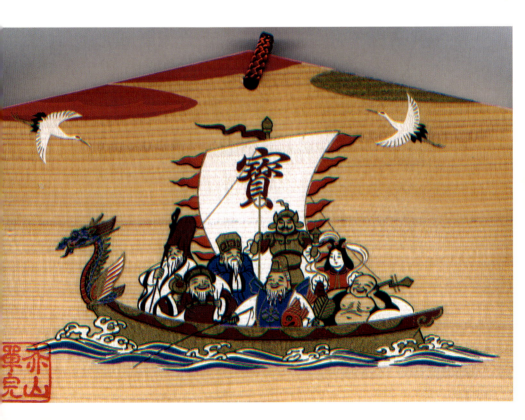

DEITIES OF KURAMA:
ALPHABETICAL LIST

NAME: Akai-gohen-zenjin
TYPE: Buddhist
LOCATION: Kurama only
LOCATION ON KURAMA: Small temple in main complex with a spring.

AKAI-GOHEN-ZENJIN IS A MINOR, local deity; and she is the spirit of the magical snake that guards the well near the main temple. Magical snakes appear in numerous Japanese legends, and can also be the alternate form of other magical creatures such as dragons. The ceiling of the shrine depicts a snake-like Oriental dragon. Magical snakes in Japanese folklore are often female, and can be either good or evil. Real snakes, including poisonous ones, exist today on Kurama, though they are not typically the kind of creatures that might spawn legends.

The full story appears on the Kyoto City Tourism and Culture website.[10] The legend tells of the monk, Buen, who was at Kurama during the Kanpyo Years, (889- 898 A.D.) He was conducting a religious service when two magic snakes appeared before him, one male and one female. The male snake tried to swallow him, and instead of reacting in fear, the monk continued to chant, but even louder. Overcome by the monk's faith, the male serpent died, and the monk was set free. The female serpent was so impressed that she swore to protect the waters that flowed from the spring on the sacred mountain. In the aftermath of this event the monk didn't know what to do with the dead body of the giant male serpent. He petitioned the Emperor for help. An imperial regiment of fifty guards was sent to cut up the serpent and bury the pieces.

The Takekiri Ceremony commemorates this event. The ceremony is performed to honor the snake guardian of the waters. Performing the ceremony is said to prevent disaster. In the ceremony two groups of people dressed as priests cut up bamboo which represents the snake. The winning team's region is favored with a better rice harvest by the gods. A two-man team must cut their bamboo into four pieces, then carry the pieces to the front of the temple. After a winner is declared, the bamboo is blessed with chants, cut into pieces, and awarded to a select few to help 'ward off' misfortune in their homes. Finally, the 'female bamboo,' with roots intact, is taken back to the area where it was dug-up and replanted.

NAME: Amida Buddha
TYPE: Buddhist
Nyorai (Buddhas)
Tendai
LOCATION ON KURAMA: The Amida Buddha is found in the Tenpōrin-dō building just below the main temple complex.

THE AMIDA BUDDHA ORIGINATES FROM INDIAN BUDDHISM. His name in Sanskrit is Amitabha and the name means "infinite light" or "infinite life." The Amida Buddha has promised to those who recite his name with sincerity, an afterlife in a 'pure land' of ultimate bliss. The Amida

Buddha is important in many schools of Buddhism. He is the key figure in the popular Pure Land 'Jodo' sects of Japanese Buddhism. Pure Land Buddhism and Nichiren Buddhism are the two most popular sects in Japan today. Zen Buddhism may be far better known to westerners, but has a relatively small following in Japan. Pure Land Buddhism was an effort to bring to the common people the possibility of enlightenment. Followers have only to chant Amida's name Namu Amida Butsu ("Hail the Amida Buddha") to receive entry into a heaven-like pure land, in which they can more easily seek enlightenment. (This sect, like most other forms of Japanese Buddhism originated in nearby Kyoto.) While Pure Land Buddhism focuses heavily on the Namu Amida Butsu chant, many Tendai and other Japanese Buddhist sects also incorporate this practice.

Statues of Nyorai can be recognized by the "snail curl" hair, simple clothing, the higher section of hair on the top section of the head called nikkei, or lump of wisdom, and the radiant spot on the forehead. The mudra, or position of the hands, on the deity is also important. The Amida Buddha of Kurama, has the Vitarka or teaching mudra position. The thumb and forefinger of each hand touch. The palm of the top hand faces outward at chest level, the other hand is palm up in the lap.

NAME: Benzaiten, Benten
TYPE: Buddhist – Originally Hindu - Sarasvati
Ten/Heavenly Kings
Tendai
LOCATION ON KURAMA: There is a small temple at the base of the stairway leading up to the main temple complex. (Pictured statue is not on Kurama Mountain.)

As with many other of the Ten, Benzaiten actually evolved from an important Hindu deity, in this case Sarasvati. As Buddhism passed through India, Tibet, China and Korea, the deities that the people already revered were incorporated into Buddhism as 'protectors of the faith.' She is the one female among Japan's Seven Lucky Gods. Benzaiten is a water goddess, often associated with rivers, oceans, lakes or streams. Her Indian name, Sarasvati, is actually the name of a river (Sarsuti) in India. She presides over three rivers in Japan, Miyajima, Chikubushima, and Enoshima. More importantly, she is a patroness of the arts, including music, dancing and acting. She is usually depicted playing a biwa (a Japanese mandolin). Talent in such things often brings luck, and thus, her inclusion among the gods of luck. Several times, the author made offerings for the successful completion of this book at the Benzaiten shrine.

Benzaiten is often depicted as a beautiful woman with the power to assume the form of a snake. Snakes are important symbols in Japan. The snake is one of the twelve Zodiac Animals. The snake and turtle are the guardians of the north.

Name: Bishamonten, Bishamon
Type: Buddhist
Ten/Heavenly King
Tendai
Location on Kurama: Bishmonten is one of Kurama's major deities. There are altars dedicated to him (and in sev-

eral of these instances, also to Kannon and Maõ-son) at the cable car station, the worship area of the main temple, the sacred room below the main temple, the museum, as well as images on lanterns outside the main temple.

BISHAMONTEN IS A GOD OF WAR AND WARRIORS. He wears armor, holds a sword in his right hand and holds a pagoda in his left. He is the most powerful of the four guardians of the compass directions. (He is the guardian of the north.) His belt often has a lion's head, symbolizing his fierce nature. Several of the Bishamonten statues at Kurama have him shading his eyes to look outward, to the south of Kurama toward Kyoto, possibly a protecting gaze to the capital. The pagoda symbolizes the divine treasure house. Bishamonten protects and distributes treasure, earning him the title of the god of wealth. Bishamonten is also associated with tigers, because he appeared in a vision to the founder of the temple on the year, day and hour of the tiger in 770 A.D.

Bishamonten is truly a 'defender of the faith.' He appears in *The Lotus Sutra* as the one who protects the Buddha when he speaks, and he always listens to the Buddha's teaching. *The Lotus Sutra* is considered by many to be the most important text in Buddhism. Bishamonten is also one of the Japanese Seven Lucky Gods. Many visitors come to Kurama Mountain on the month and the day of the tiger (in early January), because tradition says if one visits Bishamonten at this time, they will have infinite amounts of good luck. Bishamon is patron of physicians, policemen, reporters, soldiers and ambassadors.

Bishamonten is known to some as Tamonten, and in India as Kubera, or Vaisravana. At Kurama Temple, Bishamonten is considered part of the deity Sonten. Bishamonten may be accompanied by his wife Kichijoten and by Zennishi Doji. There are several notable statues of Bishamonten in the Kurama museum, including several designated by the Japanese government as Important Cultural Properties.

NAME: Fudõ
TYPE: Buddhist
Myo
Tendai
LOCATION ON KURAMA: Fudõ Myo temple

FUDÕ MYO IS THE CHIEF OF THE MYO, "KINGS OF LIGHT," or "Heavenly Kings." His role is to help people to conquer their inner demons, as Fudõ actually means "immovable in fire." He has a temple on Kurama Mountain. (Pictured statue is not on Kurama Mountain.) In Buddhist art, Fudõ is pictured with a fierce expression sitting on a rock, surrounded by flames, with a sword in one hand and a rope in the other. The 'demon-slaying sword' symbolizes wisdom, cutting through ignorance. The rope is used to bind up demons. Fudõ looks like a stylized lion or Fu dog-like being with a blue skin. The flames are said to represent the purification of the mind.

Spiritually, he is referred to as the conqueror of evil. The weapons are for slaying and binding the demons in oneself, that prevent oneself from achieving the goal of enlightenment. Fudõ can also be seen as the being who chooses to sit in the flames of life, using all of life's experiences as fuel for his enlightenment, while he sits on the immovable rock of his faith. Fudõ appears in *The Lotus Sutra*, and is very important in a number of schools of Japanese Buddhism.

CONNECTION TO KURAMA: Fudõ is a prominent deity in Tendai Buddhism, to which Kurama Temple belonged for most of its history.

QUALITIES: Fudõ has long been the patron god of samurai and Bushi warriors. They look to Fudõ for his ability to stand firm in his beliefs, and wield his weapons even when he is surrounded by the flames of pain and chaos. Fudõ is also interpreted spiritually. He is referred to as the "conqueror of evil."

SITES ASSOCIATED WITH FUDÕ: There is a large temple dedicated to Fudõ, but it is not open to the public. There is a small mandala embedded in the pathway in front of this temple, which is a great place to stand to feel its energy. Fudõ is often paired with a very similar-looking deity in red, called Aizen, the God of Love and Sexual Passion, who turns earthly desires into spiritual awakening. There is no visible sign of Aizen on Kurama, yet there have been stories of groups that associate this deity with Kurama Mountain.

NAME: Jizõ

TYPE: Buddhist Bosatsu (Bodhisattva) Tendai

LOCATION ON KURAMA: There are several temples connected to Jizõ. The largest are the ones just past the Yuki shrine, and the one between the main temple and the top of the mountain. There is a small temple at the Kibune side entrance, and there is a statue of the Six Jizõ near the nursery school.

THE BODHISATTVA JIZÕ IS THE GUARDIAN OF CHILDREN, pregnant women, travelers, lost souls and firemen. Jizõ is able to cross between the Six Realms of Existence, and is known for rescuing souls from hell and purgatory, especially the souls of unborn children. Jizō is typically pictured as a monk carrying a jewel and a staff. (This picture is not from Kurama Mountain.)

CONNECTION TO KURAMA: Jizō is an important deity in Tendai Buddhism, the sect that Kurama Mountain was a part for most of its history.

QUALITIES: Jizō is one of the most popular Bodhisattvas in Japan. Jizō is known for a number of different things, including rescuing sinners from hell and protecting children during childhood. Jizō is also the patron of pregnant women, aborted or stillborn infants, travelers, lost souls, firemen and children.

ORIGIN: Jizō is a very popular Bodhisattva in Japan. He originated in India as Kshitigarbha.

Jizō's diverse role is related to the story of how he fulfills his Bodhisatva's vow. Jizō dedicated himself to traveling into hell to rescue sinners and children, especially the unborn. Buddhist cosmology states that the souls of sinners and dead children would otherwise be stuck in hell for the eon between the death of the Gautama (historical Buddha) and the arrival of the Maitreya (future) Buddha. Women who have miscarriages or abortions in Japan will typically make an offering at a Jizō shrine to ask him to rescue the unborn child.

The three main locations of Jizō on the mountain are the Six-Jizō statue by the nursery school, the Jizō Temple just past the Yuki shrine and the Jizō shrine near the top of the mountain. There is also a small Jizō altar by the Kibune entrance to the mountain. Jizōs often come in a set of six, because of Jizō's vow to rescue souls from wherever they are in the Six Realms of Rebirth. The Six Realms are: heavenly beings, humans, warring spirits, animals, hungry ghosts and hell.

NAME: Kannon (English Name Kwan Yin (from Chinese))
TYPE: Buddhist
Bosatsu (Bodhisattva)
Tendai
LOCATIONS ON KURAMA: There is an entryway fountain and statue at the main gate, an altar in the cable car station, and a statue inside the museum. There are representations of Kannon at the main temple altar as well as beneath the main temple.

QUALITIES: Bodhisattvas are those who 'seek the wisdom of awakening' and who seek to use it to accomplish the Bodhisattva vow also embraced by serious followers of Mahayana (Northern) Buddhism. "Though there are innumerable sentient beings, I vow to save them all."

KANNON IS KNOWN AS THE GODDESS OF COMPASSION, the hearer of cries. Her Japanese name is Kannon, though she is most commonly known outside Japan by her Chinese name Kwan Yin. She is the best known of all the Bodhisattvas. The Dalai Lama is an incarnation of Kwan Yin. Kwan Yin is most often depicted as female, but can also be depicted as a male. The statues with two arms are Chinese in origin. The goddess' many-armed versions are inspired by the traditional Indian statues.

The Kannon on Kurama is a Senju Kannon, or thousand-armed-Kannon. These arms are symbolic, and each one of them holds a different object, representing a different quality of the deity. A thousand does not literally mean a thousand arms, but rather an infinite number of arms. Most thousand-

armed Kannon statues have between thirty and fifty arms.
CONNECTION TO KURAMA: In 797 A.D., the architect of the
famous Toji temple in Kyoto, saw a vision of Senju-Kannon
while meditating upon Mt. Kurama. He saw her as having the love of the moon, and built a series of temples and
pagodas on the mountain to honor her. By the end of the
tenth century, Kurama Temple was the most widely visited
Kannon Temple in the Kyoto/Osaka area. Other popular
Kannon sites of this time were Ishiyama, Kiyomizudera,
Hasedera, Tsubosakadera and Kokawadera. Other temples
were added to this group in the eleventh and twelfth centuries to make a total of thirty-three in the Kansai area.
QUALITIES: Kwan Yin is considered to be the embodiment
of compassion. On Kurama she is associated with the spirit
of the moon.
ORIGIN: Kannon arrived in Japan in the seventh century
when pilgrims returned from China with Buddhist teachings and scriptures.
SITES ASSOCIATED WITH KANNON: While many temples and
shrines to Kannon were originally built around Kurama,
none remain. As with Bishamonten, Kannon's presence is
now officially recognized on the main altars of the temple
as part of the trinity, however, the fountain of Kannon near
the temple's entrance, is the only place on the mountain
dedicated solely to her.

NAME: Miroku Bosatsu (Sanskrit
Maitreya)
TYPE: Buddhist Bodhisattva
(In Tendai, & Shingon Buddhism, may
also be a Nyorai)
LOCATION ON KURAMA: There is a

small Maitreya temple located on the path between the upper cable car station and the main path.(Picture not taken on Kurama)

M IROKU BOSATSU IS THE FUTURE BUDDHA, whose presence can be felt on earth now, but will not live on earth until 5,670,000,000 years after the death of the historical Buddha. At that time Miroku will appear in the world and save all beings who have not yet reached enlightenment. At that time, a flower known as the Dragon Blossom will bloom, and Miroku will convene a gathering three-times, to preach the teaching to save the world. This is called the "Three Gatherings of the Dragon Blossom."

The Buddha of the Future is not a solemn figure. Miroku Bosatsu is known as the friendly, loving or laughing Buddha. Before he became fully enlightened, he would stand outside the gates of the city and meditate on loving-kindness. His contemplation was so powerful that those who passed by experienced the great love of the universe. He is known for leading people towards enlightenment by encouraging spiritual discipline, concentration and wisdom. Some sources state that Hotei, the Laughing Buddha and Chinese God of Luck, with the big belly, is an incarnation of Miroku Bosatsu.

NAME: Maõ-son
TYPE: Buddhist
Kurama only
LOCATION ON KURAMA: Cable car station-altar, Main Altar, Under Temple, Õsugi Gongen and Okunoin Museum.

Maõ-son is a major local deity. Maõ-son is considered to be a warrior god from the planet Venus, who came to earth to help mankind. Tendai Buddhism connects him to the Indian Buddhist deity Vajrayaksa, whose Japanese name is Kongoyashi. Kongoyashi is one of the Myo, the "Kings of Light."

Maõ-son is portrayed in two different ways. In written accounts of his origin, he is eternally sixteen years-old, and appears human. The statues of him in the basement of the Kurama Temple and in Kõmyõshinden, however, show him as a stout, bearded, middle-aged man with wings. The stout appearance seems appropriate for a god of earth, reflecting his stability and power. The wings reflect his extraterrestrial origin, and his ability to cross between planets.

History and Origins: According to one of the books of the temple "In ancient prehistoric times, a tremendous sound from the sky shook the ground, and thousands of balls of fire rained down. A tornado of fire appeared in the sky. From out of this tornado came a revolving object, transparent, but white with heat. It looked somewhat like a UFO, but was actually the heavenly vehicle of the great, spiritual God of the Universe, Maõ-son. He landed on Kurama Mountain as a messenger from the planet Venus, directed by the order of Heaven. He became the divine ruler of spirit. This was 6.5 million years ago, and is the true beginning of religion on Kurama, as has been revealed to people over time." [11]

Another believer who wanted to have such a vision, prayed at Okunoin, with great spiritual intensity in the 1500's. The next morning the person saw a vision of Maõ-son in a spider web and carved a statue of what he saw.[12] The artist was Karino Hogan Motonobu (1476-1559)[13] who worked for the Ashikaga Shogun. The image was enshrined at Okunoin and is only shown once every sixty years, in the year of the Hinoe-tora (fire-tiger). The last year of the fire-tiger was 1986. (The next will be 2046) There is a long tradition in Japan of connecting the energy of new or local deities to more widely known deities. From the Sanskrit symbol used to represent him, it is clear Maō-son has been associated with the Indian deity Vajrayaksa, also known in Japan as Kongoyashi.

Kongoyashi is one of the Five Kings of Radiant Wisdom, and is often connected with the Niō, the guardians of the Buddhist temple. Kongoyashi's purpose is to protect the Buddhist Dharma (universal laws, teachings of the Buddha), to destroy enemies who oppose Dharma, and the forceful guidance of sentient beings on the path to enlightenment. There may also be some connection with the Burmese deity Ko myo shin.

Maō-son looks like the Kurama Tengu, though some have denied this. I suspect that he is the more spiritual form of deity behind the ancient legend of the Tengu. Even the tree Osugi Gongen, that is considered by today's Kurama Temple to have been an incarnation of Maō-son, was reported in the Kyoto Guide of 1895 to be the mysterious home of the Tengu.[14]

QUALITIES: Maō-son seeks to help both individuals and all of mankind to progress spiritually. He helps people overcome their faults and vices to become enlightened through courage and understanding of the genuine self. Maō-son's role is to guide the evolution of all beings on earth, not just mankind, but also the gods, nature spirits and all other beings on earth. He is a powerful protector, and he helps those who are suffering from sin and sadness to be guided towards virtue and happiness.[15]

According to an ancient legend in the Kuki family, a meteorite from Venus fell to Japan. It broke into three pieces high in the sky. One fell north of the Kyoto/Kurama area, and is said to be enshrined as the Maō-son meteorite at Okunoin. Maō-den, the second one, fell in the Kumano/Kishu area, and the third, remaining one, fell on Mt. Takamikura.

NAME: Sonten
TYPE: Buddhist
Kurama only
LOCATION ON KURAMA: Sonten is name and concept of deity unique to Kurama Buddhism. Sonten is the sacred cosmos, the unified energy of Maō-son, Bishamonten, and Kannon. Sonten is a logical extension of the early vision of Bishamonten and Kannon as emanations of the same deity.

HISTORY AND ORIGINS: As a deity representing "All That Is" there is no pictorial representation of Sonten. Sonten represents all that is. The name Sonten translates as "respectable heaven." Sonten represents deity as all that is. From one of the Kurama temple's books:

ALL EXISTS IN SONTEN. All exists as part of Sonten. All means all visible things and invisible things. It includes all in existence in the universe, all creatures, all feelings, and all that exists in the hearts and minds of mankind, all of the stars at night, all the things seen in the daylight. It includes everything seen in the universe, all of the electromagnetic spectrum.[17]

CONNECTION TO KURAMA: Sonten, which translates to "Respectable Heaven" is a conception of God as "the great original soul" or "All That Is." The name "Sonten" and this particular idea of deity originated on Kurama; it did not come from traditional Buddhism.

SITES ASSOCIATED WITH: As a transcendent deity, Sonten is considered to be part of every temple/shrine on Kurama Mountain.

SITES ON KURAMA

THERE ARE MORE SITES ON KURAMA CONNECTED to Maõ-son than to any other deity. The waterfall, not far above the information office and cable car station, is dedicated to Maõ-son. Two of the most powerful energy places on the mountain are connected to Maõ-son -- the Õsugi Gongen tree (considered a reincarnation of Maõ-son) and the Inner Temple, which is where Maõ-son is said to have landed on earth.

MAÕ-SON AS ASCENDED MASTER SANAT KUMARA
Alice Bailey (1880-1949) and Madame H. P. Blatvaksy (1831-1891) were instrumental in spreading the knowledge of and world-view of a brotherhood of "Ascended Masters" that watches over the earth. Madame Blavatsky was one of the founders of the Theosophical Society. (1877) Alice Bailey was a long-term, active member. Their writings continue to influence much of New Age thought today. Their writings were based on an inclusive mixture of all of the religious traditions known at the time, coalesced into a cohesive whole with their own channeled materials. These religious traditions included Christianity, Judaism, Buddhism and Hinduism. Current New Age thought often makes mention of the "Ascended Masters" described in this material, including St. Germaine, Kwan Yin, Melchizidek, Jesus, and Maitreya.

ONE JAPANESE REIKI teacher
WROTE IN A STUNNING OBSERVATION:
"When you talk about Reiki with a capital "R" it is the energy found by Usui Mikao, through his 'satori' on Kurama-yama, under the influence of GohoMaõ-son, also known as Ascended Master Sanat Kumara." (GohoMaõ-son is another form of the name Maõ-son.) Several esoteric websites[16]

describe Sanat Kumara as "The Lord of the World." They say that he is "the etheric/physical expression of our Planetary Logos, who dwells on Shambala. This is a great being, originally from Venus, who sacrificed himself to become the personality vehicle for the ensouling deity of our planet eighteen and a half million years-ago. He is the nearest aspect of God that we can know."

Reiki Note

MAÕ-SON AS POWER OF EARTH: While it cannot be proven, Maõ-son may be connected to the Reiki power symbol. Maõ-son is a peculiar blend of earth and fire, which is connected to the elemental power of the earth. The Reiki power symbol has a similar fire and earth quality to it. Maõ-son's overall mission to protect and guide mankind fits in well with the essence of Reiki: to heal and teach mankind.

KI NOTES: MAÕ-SON MEDITATION: Imagine you are there when Maõ-son's energy first came to earth. Imagine sitting upon a sleeping volcano (Kurama is volcanic), and looking into the sky, seeing what he saw: the rain of balls of fire coming from the sky, the tornado of fire. Imagine the god striding across the earth. Ayumi, who has done much of the Japanese research for this book, says that several Japanese articles refer to this association between Maõ-son and Kumara.

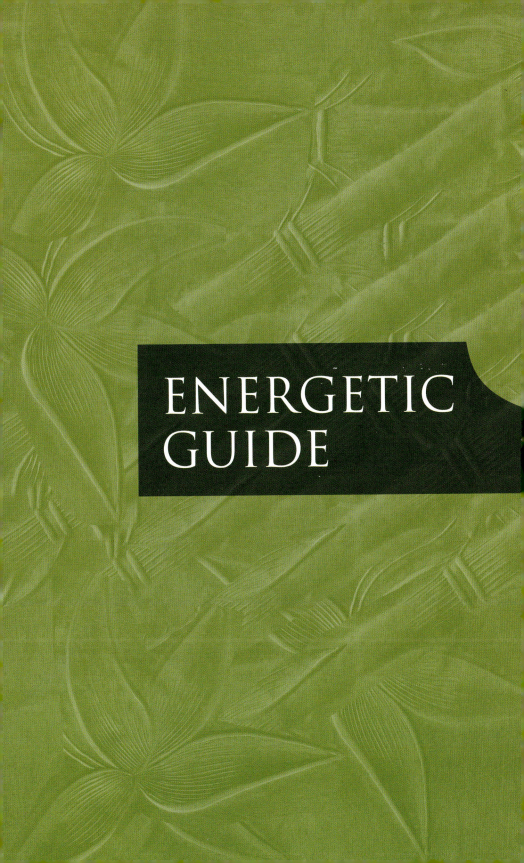

ENERGETIC
GUIDE

Kurama Mountain
is an Energy Playground

In this chapter you will find a series of exercises and games designed to enhance your awareness of your psychic, or perceptive, abilities and experiences. Exploring the sacred world is a form of divine play and it is important to remember, as you play, you are in a process of discovery. Exercises and games, such as those presented here, can be played or practiced on Mt. Kurama, or at any other sacred place or power spot. In the early phases of developing intuition and connecting to the mountain, it is difficult to be certain if one is 'making it up' or if one is experiencing a real, but subtle phenomenon. The difference between making something up and discovery has more to do with willingness to share perceptions and see if others agree or disagree than about absolute reality.

Also it is important to remember that people's perceptions do vary. Feeling energy fields is similar to the old story of the blind men who feel the elephant, and then try to explain it. One feels the tail; one feels the leg; one feels the trunk. Is it any wonder that they disagree? Different people are sensitive to different energy frequencies, and perceive the world in different psychic ways. Some are visual, some are kinesthetic, some are auditory, some just know things. Like all other kinds of natural abilities, most people have some skills they are naturally best at, and other skills will improve with practice. Attending Reiki classes and regular practice of Reiki can help strengthen one's psychic abilities.

In this type of exploration, your greatest assets can be an open mind, the ability to have fun as you play and explore, and a willingness to be wrong. The purpose of these games is to allow the participant to focus on the energy of the mountain.

Many hikers just climb up one end and down the other, none the wiser about the powerful place they have walked through. Those who live in nearby Kurama village and those who work every day on the mountain are also not affected by the power of the mountain. The power of the mountain pertains to the visitor focusing on the right set of frequencies, similar to the way a radio is focused or 'tuned' to the correct frequency to hear any sound at all. For some the energy of the mountain is subtle, for many others it is not subtle at all. It is recommended to play these games sparingly on the way up the mountain, and experiment more on the journey down. If one is over energized, it is very difficult to focus on subtle energies, or to ground on this mountain. Moving, eating and grounding exercises can be helpful, but the only real solution is to get off the mountain.

DIFFERENT APPROACHES TO A SACRED PLACE

Different people have varying goals or intentions when visiting sacred places. This chapter contains exercises to suit all types of explorers. These exercises can be practiced at any sacred place to offer the visitor a deeper connection to the heart of the area. Prior practice of these techniques in a variety of places will serve the visitor well when they come to the mountain, and begin to appreciate the power of Kurama Mountain. A traditional Buddhist approach is to use the energy of a place as a springboard to achieving higher enlightenment. Buddhists focus on meditating by emptying the mind, or focusing by keeping the mind on sacred syllables. They pray to their deities, light incense and candles.

A different approach used by many more earth-centered philosophies is to actually try to speak to the spirit of the place. The visitor respectfully goes to the sacred place and says "Hello, I am _____. Who are you?" Such people seek to commune with the spirit or spirits of the place. Still others approach a sacred place as an abstract place of power. They tend to focus on exploring the energetic aspects of the space. Most of the games in this chapter are NOT traditional to Japan, or to anywhere else. However, activities similar to these do appear in different cultures. Activities that are traditional are described as such in the text.

HANDS ENERGIZING EXERCISES

EARTH GAMES

Earth games are exercises that involve connecting to the energy of the earth surfaces on Kurama Mountain or other places.

EARTH BOUNCE

The earth in different areas has a different energetic feel to it. An energy ball from the hands is bounced against the ground and the results are observed. This same technique can be done sideways in houses or other buildings to measure the relative amount of energy flow through walls, windows, doorways and mirrors.

- Energize the hands to create an energy ball.
- 'Bounce' the energy ball down towards the ground.
- Observe what happens; repeat over different surfaces, at different angles.
- Note your results.

The lower the energy of a place, the more the energy ball seems to simply hit the ground with a thud. In higher energy places, the ground has a different quality. The energy goes some distance into the earth, and some of it bounces back to the surface. The difference is especially clear when playing with two adjacent surfaces. Bouncing the energy off a road will feel different than bouncing the energy off the earth, bouncing the energy off concrete will feel different than off natural stone. Bouncing energy off a riverbank will feel different than bouncing off the river.

Earth: Far Feeling

In high-energy places, one may be able to sense energy much farther away than normal.

- Energize hands to create an energy ball.
- Face the mountain, scan around, and see if you can get a sense of the shape of the bulk of the mountain. How far away does the energetic horizon seem to be?
- Try repeatedly in different areas and see if it is easier in some areas than others.

Energy Current Games: Turn Around

There are energy currents that go up and down slopes, especially in high energy places. Few of the world's power spots are flat.

- Stand somewhere where there is a definite slope. Ideally, stand midway on the slope so there is part of the slope above and below.
- Turn slowly in place.
- Notice how the energy feels from the uphill direction and from the downhill direction.

There is a definite current of energy that runs down hill, and a second current that runs uphill. These rivers of energy can be felt, but standing or walking in the same direction tends to desensitize the body. Turning in place allows a person to perceive the differences in the energy that surrounds them.

Energy Current Games: Moving Backward vs. Forward

Everyone is wired a little differently. Most people are far more protected energetically on the front of their body then on the back. Because of this, it may be easier for some to feel energy when moving backward than when moving forward. This exercise can be used when walking through a high energy area, or better yet by sitting in the train or cable car with one's back facing the direction you are traveling in. Much of Kurama Mountain is uneven. Because of the unevenness of the terrain, hiking backward except for short stretches is not recommended.

ENERGY CURRENT GAMES: FINDING THE 'RIGHT' SPOT

Kurama Mountain has hundreds of energy spots of different sizes and types. Finding them has a great deal to do with awareness and willingness to move slowly and experiment. Finding them is helped by paying attention to what in the area may be contributing to the existence of the power spot. Many of the exercise/games in this section are the result of the willingness to experiment and play. All of the temples and shrines on Kurama Mountain are at power spots on the mountain. However, a way to find the best spot is to go to one of these sites, and walk slowly around the area. For me, the strongest 'power spots' are not the exact place where people stand to pray, or at the site itself, but nearby. Also because different people are sensitive to different energies, individuals will vary in which location is the best for them.

To find these spots:

- Walk around the area at about 1/4 speed. Act like you're an ordinary tourist looking around.
- Notice if you feel any differences in your body, or in your sense of the world around you.

When you find a potential spot, try to find its edge. Put one leg inside the spot and one leg outside, and shift your weight and your torso side to side. Notice any differences.

- Spend time standing on this spot, 'absorbing the energy.'
- Give thanks to the area, and depart.

One of my favorite spots is near the trees of the Yuki Shrine.

Sitting there is like feeling a thin stream of water hitting and semi-hollowing out the top of the head. Another of my favorite spots is at the side of the winding path, near the ends of one of the hairpin turns; there is an old stump, where I feel the energy coming up through my feet.

Magnify Intention

The following activities are other more formal ways to approach Kurama Mountain, and things one can spend time doing there. The high-energy field of sacred places can be used as a megaphone to magnify the power of your intentions. The following are some ideas for how to do this.

Life Contemplation and Planning

Kurama is an excellent place to contemplate the direction of one's life, give thanks for blessings, and make requests for what is really important in this life.

Requesting Assistance from Kurama's Deities

Kurama's power also makes it a good place to request divine assistance. All deities are welcome on Kurama Mountain. Those wishing to pray silently to Jesus, to Mother/Father God, or however they are accustomed to praying, are all welcome. Just as Buddhists would be welcome to come and pray at a Christian sacred place, the reverse is true here.

Read a List of Names

Before going to Kurama Mountain, create a list for people who would like to receive energy sent to them on Kurama Mountain.[18]

Chanting the Heart Sutra

Occasionally the visitor will encounter individuals or groups of people chanting a long series of syllables. Usually the people doing so will visit each of the sacred places on the mountain in turn and repeat the same series. Out of politeness to other visitors to the mountain, it is NOT recommended to chant non-Buddhist prayers aloud on the mountain where others can hear, unless a Japanese-speaking member of your group has obtained permission.

Chanting is a way of clearing the mind by filling it. The syllables give the mind a focus. The sacred sounds of the syllables resonate deeply into the mind and body and create an area of higher energy. The length of the chant ensures that the individual remains at the sacred spot long enough for the energy of that spot to work with them.

One of the most common (and shorter) prayers to be chanted on Kurama is the Heart Sutra. The syllables are chanted quickly with an even emphasis:

Maka Hannya Haramitta Shingyo[19]

KAN JI ZAI BO-SA GYO. JIN HAN NYA HA RA MITA. JI SHO
KEN GO ON KAI KU. DO IS SAI KUYAKU. SHA RI SHI. SHIKI
FU I KU. KU FU I SHIKI. SHIKI SOKU ZE KU. KU SOKU ZE SHIKI.
JU SO GYO SHIKI. YAKU BU NYO ZE. SHA RI SHI. ZE SHO HO
KU SO. FU SHO FU METSU. FU KU FU JO. FU ZO FU GEN. ZE
KO KU CHU. MU SHIKI MU JU SO GYO SHIKI. MU GEN NI BI
ZETS SHIN NI. MU SHIKI SHO KO MI SOKU HO. MU GEN KAI
NAI-SHI MU I SHIKI KAI. MU MU MYO YAKU MU MU MYO JIN.
NAI SHI MU RO SHI. YAKU MU RO SHI JIN. MU KU SHU METSU
DO. MU CHIYAKU MU TOKU. I MU SHO TO KO. BO DAI SATTA.
E HAN NYA HA RA MITA KO. SHIN MU KEI GE. MU KEI GE KO.
MU U KU FU. ON RI IS SAITEN DO MU SO. KU GYO NE HAN.
SAN ZE SHO BUTSU. E HANNYA HA RA MITA. KO TOKU
A NOKU TA RA SAN MYAKU SAN BO DAI. KO CHI HAN
NYA HA RA MITA. ZE DAI JIN SHU. ZE DAI MYO SHU. ZE MU
JO SHU. ZE MU TO DO SHU. NO JO IS SAI KU SHIN JITSU FU
KO. KO SETSU HAN NYA HARA MITA SHU. SOKU SETSU SHU
WATSU: GYA TE. GYA TE. HARA GYA TE. HARA SO GYA TE.

BO DI SOWA KA. HAN NYA SHIN GYO.

Maha Prajna Paramita Heart Sutra

*Avalokitesvara Bodhisattva, doing deep prajna paramita,
clearly saw emptiness of all the five conditions,*

*Thus, completely relieving misfortune and pain. O Shariputra, form
is no other than emptiness; emptiness is no other than form;*

Form is exactly emptiness, emptiness is exactly form;

Sensation, conception, discrimination, awareness are likewise like this.

O Shariputra, all dharmas are forms of emptiness, not born, not destroyed;

Not stained, not pure, without loss, without gain;

*So in emptiness there is no form, no sensation,
conception, discrimination, awareness;*

*No eye, ear, nose, tongue, body, mind; No color,
sound, smell, taste, touch, phenomena;*

*No realm of sight . . . no realm of consciousness;
No ignorance and no end to ignorance . . .*

*No old age and death, and no end to old age and death; No suffering,
no cause of suffering, no extinguishing, no path;
No wisdom and no gain. No gain and thus.*

*The bodhisattva lives prajna paramita with no hindrance in the mind,
no hindrance, therefore no fear,*

*Far beyond deluded thoughts, this is nirvana. All past, present, and future
Buddhas live prajna paramita, And, therefore, attain anuttarasamyak-
sambodhi. Therefore know, prajna paramita is the great mantra, the vivid
mantra, the best mantra, the unsurpassable mantra;*

*It completely clears all pain; this is the truth, not a lie.
So set forth the Prajna Paramita Mantra.*

Set forth this mantra and say: Gate! Gate! Paragate! Parasamgate!

Bodhi svaha.

Prajna Heart Sutra.

Just Spending Time

The way I know when my guides are speaking is usually when something comes into my head that is odd enough, that I know I would not have ever thought of it myself. Then, through an internal question and answer period I work my way towards the intent behind the comment. Once when I was planning to go to Ōsugi Gongen and was despairing about my lack of ability to sit in meditation, I heard in my head, "Why don't you bring a book?" Spending time is more important than exactly what the visitor does on the mountain, though all of the games and activities described in this chapter have value.

Visual Games

The energy of the mountain can be enjoyed many ways. For some visitors it is visual. Their way of communing with the mountain is to look at it.

Taking Pictures

Taking pictures is an excellent way to visually connect with the energy of the mountain. Photography forces the photographer to look at the world a little differently. Focusing on what looks good in a frame encourages the visitor to notice the world in a different way. Many of the photos taken on the mountain are also energetically active. When displayed on the computer screen or printed in a book, an energy sensitive person can feel the energy emanating from the picture. There is a great pleasure in creating one's own favorite energetically active pictures.

Looking for Faces in Bark or Stone

Another game many enjoy is to look for faces or interesting shapes in the bark of trees and the roughness of natural stone. This is in many ways similar to cloud gazing. Some people use this as a means of fortune telling, asking a question and seeing what shapes or images appear in response. Others use it as a way to look for 'spirits' in the natural world. Either way this type of looking gives the visitor a different way to focus on the natural beauty around. It tends to connect the viewer more deeply to his or her environment... and it is fun.

Looking for Auras

It is easier to see the energy fields of people, trees, and high-energy areas in a high-energy field like Kurama Mountain. To try to see auras, look at the area around a person, preferably against a single-color background such as the sky or the wall of a temple.

Tree Games

Trees are important on a mountain like Kurama. There are many energetic 'games' one can play with trees.

Trees and High Energy Spots

Trees are long-lived living things. Some of the older trees on Kurama are over 1000 years-old. Existing that long in a sacred place, the tree itself concentrates the energy of the area. I had been on Kurama Mountain over thirty-five times before I noticed that many of the highest energy spots I found on the mountain occurred near these ancient trees. The roots of a given tree extend out 10-15 yards from the trunk. It is within this root ball area that these energy spots occur.

Tree Growth Affected by Energy Fields

Tree growth is affected by prolonged exposure to high-energy fields. For people who are less energetically sensitive, looking for odd tree growth patterns is a great way for locating high-energy spots. On Kurama Mountain, tree limbs grow together, tree branches twist and turn, and odd root patterns create arches that look like doorways to another world.

TALKING TO TREES

Many people talk to trees. In the Japanese religion of Shinto, many of the oldest trees are considered to be gods and are surrounded with spirit ropes. People will pray to these trees as manifestations of deity. While I do not personally pray to trees, I do like to 'talk' to them. I cannot say that they literally talk back, but often I get a sense of communication. Talking to trees is very rewarding in that it helps put life into perspective. To the eldest trees of Kurama, the life of a human being is quite short. All of our individual problems of the moment seem small and far away compared to the eloquence of time and seasons that a tree enjoys.

The clearest communication I have is with one of the trees at the Yuki shrine. The tree is right next to the path. I mentally asked the tree for permission to touch it, and was quite startled to hear the tree say "no", and then... something almost like a chuckle. In fact, every time I have asked that tree for permission to touch it, it has said "no." The tree 'likes' me just fine. When I wanted to touch the tree for a picture, the tree happily gave permission. It just really enjoys the novelty of someone asking permission. Or perhaps it was just having someone take "no" for an answer!

On a more recent visit, I told one of the people I brought to Japan, who talks to trees, to ask permission before touching it. He was given permission! Politeness is the key that opens all doors. If you believe that a tree is alive and to some degree sentient, it is only polite to ask permission before approaching, touching or hugging it. Leaning against a tree can also be an amazing experience. One's energy seems to meld with the tree. Feel the energy rising skyward, or running deep into the Earth. There are magnificent cedar trees at the top of Kurama Mountain. The soil around these trees is eroded to such an extent that a hand can be placed between the earth and the roots. The energy is strong enough here, that when a hand is placed in this spot the green energy of the tree can be felt crossing the palm.

Trees as Verticals

The energy of an area tends to flow almost like water. There is a current that tends to go from earth to sky, and another, typically easier to feel, that goes from sky to earth. This energy tends to flow down off of objects. The energy flow is strongest 3-8 feet away from the trunk of the tallest trees. This is especially clear at the trees of the Yuki shrine.

To find the flow, stand near one of these great trees, and pretend to slowly wander around and gaze at the scenery. Pay attention to how the crown of the head feels. When in the right location, it will feel like energy is slowly pouring or dripping into the visitor's crown chakra. Standing here too long may result in a headache from too much energy coming into the crown. To me it feels like the energy is slowly filling a bowl at the top of my head, and that the longer I stand in this position, the bigger the bowl on my head gets.

Water Games

There are many small water sources on Kurama and many opportunities for 'games' with water.

Purification Shrine

There are many purification shrines on Kurama. Although the Purification shrine is originally part of Shinto, it has been become part of Japanese Buddhism. Some of the purification shrines are very formal structures with dragon water spouts, roofs and stone basins. Others are just small spring fed pools beside the trail. They can be identified as purification shrines by the ladles that lie beside them.

CHI OF RUNNING WATER

There is a great deal of running water on Kurama, especially after a rain storm. A small creek runs beside the path on the lower part of the mountain. Rivulets of water stream down beside the winding path. All of this water has a high concentration of chi. On the winding path section of the trail, after a rainstorm, a small rivulet of water runs to one side of the path. Part way up, it crosses the path and runs along the other side. Walk the trail, holding one hand 'nonchalantly' over the moving water and parallel to it. The chi of the moving water will activate the chi of the hands.

STANDING OVER RUNNING WATER

Moving water is a great purifier. There are several places on Kurama Mountain where the visitor can stand over water. Many report a sense of their energy field being cleared, especially on the lower half of their body. There is a heightened sense of awareness of the Earth Star chakra being cleansed about 20 to 40 inches below the feet. This external chakra connects the individual to the grounded energy of the Earth.

THE WATER 'FALLS'

There are two waterfalls just past the cable car station on the way up Kurama Mountain. They are not what most people would consider to be waterfalls. The water shoots out of a cement culvert, and falls to the earth below. There is a traditional Japanese meditation technique of standing beneath waterfalls like these in midwinter, often for hours, and letting the water strike them upon the head to create enlightenment. One individual I spoke to said this tradition originally came from India, and that the practitioners would work up to it gradually, first by pouring a pitcher of water over the head, and then slowly increasing the amount of water and the amount of time the practitioner can stand there, before trying it for hours beneath a waterfall in mid-winter.

I do not advocate standing beneath the falls at mid-winter. However, I do think doing so on a hot summer day sounds quite pleasant. Listening to the waterfalls is another marvelous way to meditate. These waterfalls are under variable pressure. They often seem to almost talk to the visitor as they spurt and pause, flow strongly and then dwindle to a trickle in the space of a minute.

VERTICALS, EAVES AND POSTS

The shape of the objects in a high-energy environment affects the way the energy flows in that environment.

DONOR POSTS

Many parts of the trail leading up Kurama Mountain are lined with donor posts. These granite posts mention the amount of the donation and the name of the donor. These posts concentrate the energy of the area. The visitor can place his or her hands a few inches over the posts, and slowly move the hands from side to side to feel the energy concentrated by these vertical posts. This is a very good technique for activating and strengthening the amount of energy coming out of the palms. The visitor can also move the hands over the path, over the post, then over the ground on the other side to better appreciate the differences in energy. The amount and type of energy felt over these posts varies from place to place. Since the posts are identical, the only differences in the energy felt are the result of the exact area on the mountain where the posts are found.

EAVES

The roofs of Japanese temples and shrines have a very distinctive slight curve. The shape of these roofs channels the energy from the sky. The energy is typically strongest 12-24 inches away from the building, as the energy soars off the roof and towards the ground. To feel this effect, stand close to the building, and slowly move outward, until the falling energy is sensed the most strongly.

TORII

Torii are the symbols of Shinto. They consist of two upright stone or wood beams, with two cross beams overhead. In Shinto, the original torii is said to have been a 'rooster perch.' It is a reference to one of the creation stories of Japan, of how the sun goddess was lured forth from her cave by the crow of the rooster. The torii looks more like a doorway however. Typically, torii are found near the entrance to Shinto shrines. Sometimes visitors walk through torii, sometimes they walk around them. In one traditional game, you make a wish and toss a small pebble up into the air, and try to get it to land on the torii. If it lands on the torii, tradition says the wish will come true. This is typically a children's game.

Another game for Reiki people to do is to use the torii as a gateway of blessing. Common choices for intentions are: "May I be blessed with stronger intuition." "May I be blessed with love." Or, "May I be blessed with the energy of the mountain." The practitioner approaches the torii and mentally asks permission. Then discreetly draws or intends Reiki symbols in the area framed by the torii. State the intention three times, and then very slowly walk through the torii. Many can feel the energy of the blessing held by the torii shape.

SMALL SPIRIT GAMES

There are many energies, great and small, at a sacred place such as Kurama. Many of the small energies are the natural energies generated by energetically powerful places. Some cultures refer to these as fairies or leprechauns. I tend to sense them as small energy balls, ranging in size from a pea to a basketball.

Hello Scan

These energies are typically casually friendly. If the visitor says hello, they will often say hello back. It is similar to what happens if a boat goes by the shore. There is a natural tendency for the people on the boat to wave, and for the people on the shore to wave back. The intention is sort of "I see you, and I'm on a boat" and "I see you and you're on a boat." Energetically I find when I say hello, I can get a sense for how many energies are in the area, and where they are, based on the sense of "hellos" I get back. Other visitors may be able to see that some areas of the woods are brighter, or just have a sense of knowing. Other more psychic visitors may be able to have conversations with these energies, or even photograph them.

Spirit of the Mountain Games

Where to go Today

Kurama Mountain is always happy to have visitors, especially energy-aware visitors who hike the mountain. If one befriends a sacred place, and begins to know many great areas, then it becomes a dual question of: (1.) Where does the visitor want to go today? (2.) Where does the mountain want the visitor? There is a sense of the mountain itself inviting the visitor to one location versus another.

Scan of the Mountain

In a high-energy field, there is a different sense of scope, of reach, psychically, than in less high-energy areas. One subjective measure of how the visitors' energy interacts with the energy of the space is the sense of sweep, the sense of how far beyond the reach of the fingers do they feel a certain degree of connection. While on the mountain (and to try it, at different locations off it), reach out your hand and pass it at arms length from left to right. Some get an almost tactile sense of the ground past their hand. Some get an almost radar like 'ping,' some get a sense of bulk. Some get no sense at all. It is useful when practicing this kind of exercise to start some place where there are major differences in the shape of the land in different directions.

AFTER YOU THINK IT'S OVER: MOUNTAIN GAMES

Visitors who treat Kurama as a sacred place on their visit frequently find that the effects of their visit become apparent after they come down from the mountain, and sometimes days, weeks, or months later.

LEAVING KURAMA: COMING DOWN FROM ORDINARY

If the visitor stays on the mountain for a period of hours, especially if they stay in one general area, their energy acclimates to the energy level of the mountain. The energy of the mountain begins to feel quite ordinary. There are trees, dirt, ferns and leaves. Reiki people often feel little desire to actually do Reiki, and little awareness of the energy in their hands. It is in getting off the mountain that the difference between the power spot on Kurama, and the ordinary Kyoto energy becomes apparent. A fish in a bowl is not really aware of the water around it. After coming down from the mountain, it is as if the water is being let out of the bowl. There seems to be a different quality in the air which highlights how extraordinary Kurama's "ordinary" reality really is.

CRANKINESS: A SYMPTOM OF ENERGETIC OVERLOAD

For someone in moderately good shape, Kurama Mountain is

not a big hike. It is a small mountain in size, less than 2000 feet. The hike up and down Kurama is about 1000 feet in elevation, and can easily be done in 3 to 4 hours, with time added for meditation and sightseeing. However, it is very normal for energetically aware visitors to be very tired at the end of the day, and even cranky. Just like small children at Disneyland can be tired and cranky from too much stimulation, so too can adults grow weary from spending the day in a high-energy field, especially if they do many of the exercises in this book! There is nothing wrong with overload, just be as kind as you can to your fellow travelers, get off the mountain, and perhaps encourage people to have an early night.

ENERGY SURGES

Another phenomena that may occur to visitors who have spent time on the mountain are energy surges. These may occur any time from the time of their visit to 2 to 3 months later. Especially for Reiki people, there is a sense of receiving an energetic attunement from the mountain. These surges can happen anywhere, typically when the visitor is at rest and focused on something else. I have experienced them on the subway to Osaka, in the movie theater and at night when trying to sleep. Since Reiki activates the energy in the palm chakras to the point where it is useful for healing, it is not surprising that the majority of the energy surge occurs there.

Other times the surges focus on the back of the hand, the third eye and crown, and even the soles of the feet. There is often a sense of white light in the third eye, almost uncomfortably bright. I attribute much of the growth in the quality of Reiki energy that comes through my hands, and the strengthening of my psychic abilities in the last few years, to my time on Kurama Mountain.

Meditating on the Photographs

Kurama is a mountain of great energy. Even photographs of the mountain have a certain power. Many people who have seen the photographs in this book report feeling positive, often healing energies coming from these pictures. Different pictures have different types and levels of energy. This book has been designed so that the pictures seem to have captured the energy of the mountain, and to continue to be connected to it.

The most common sensation reported is a shift in the feeling of heat or vibration in the hands as they are slowly passed over the pictures. Others feel coolness, almost like a breeze either in their forehead or heart, or even on the outside of the arm. Others have a sense of brightness or light. Page through the book, looking for a picture that attracts you to its energy. Some of the best photographs for meditation are Ōsugi Gongen, The Amida Buddha, the Yuki Shrine and Okunoin. To activate the pictures of the mountain, either use the Reiki distance symbol or use visualization to connect to the energy of that place on the mountain. Spend five to ten minutes in meditation, asking for the peace and serenity of the mountain to fill you. Give thanks, and make a few notes on your experiences. Notice how the experience varies from time to time, even when using the same picture.

Physical Factors affecting Sacred Places

Kurama Mountain's size and variety make it an excellent place to explore the different factors that affect the energy of a sacred place. Geology can have a profound effect on the energy of an area. Seven million years ago, Kurama Mountain and its environs were flat, part of an ancient shallow sea. Volcanoes thrust up through the sea floor, forming the range of mountains that surround Kyoto. The oldest rocks on Kurama Mountain are the remains of the ancient seabed, and they are near the base. The energies in this area tend to be small and numerous, and differ in character from the larger energies near the top.

Topology also has an influence on the energy currents. Many of the energy areas on the mountain are where the energy rises or descends steep ravines, such as the pathway by the Upper Cable Car and Pagoda. On the winding path, passing one's hands over the donor posts by the side of the pathway also concentrates the energy. Other energy concentrators are the eaves of the buildings. When standing at the edge of the eaves of Kurama's temples, many feel a curtain of Ki energy pouring down.

There is also a strong correlation between perceived high-energy spots, and the presence of trees with odd growth patterns nearby. The trees concentrate the natural Ki of the earth. For centuries, one of the most famous and powerful locations on Kurama was Ōsugi Gongen. Ōsugi Gongen is named for the giant tree of the same name that stood here for centuries until blown over in a typhoon in 1950. The tree was considered a reincarnation of Maō-son. It was in this spot that Mikao Usui meditated for twenty-one days before receiving the enlightenment experience that led to Reiki. Even now there are benches in the area for people or groups of people to sit, eat lunch or meditate.

Trash can also affect the energy of the temples and shrines on the mountain. During the prime weeks of the fall foliage season in mid-November an overwhelming number of hikers from all over Japan come into the mountains. Cigarette butts and other trash may be left in some of the places where typically people light candles and light incense. This creates a definite heaviness or prickliness to the energy of the area, as if the spirit of the area is displeased. The staff of the temple will typically take care of this daily. However, if a visitor is determined to make an offering at such a place, try the following. Remove the offending objects, placing them into a small plastic trash bag to take with you off the mountain. Then, if a purification basin is nearby, ladle its water onto the shrine, or sweep off the shrine to purify it. Prayers should be offered to apologize for the obstruction, and for the energies of the area to re-bless the shrine. If the energy of the area lightens, then candles or incense can be lit.

THE SACRED ENERGIES OF KURAMA MOUNTAIN

Over a thousand years of chanting and devotion have strengthened the energies of the mountain. This is especially noticeable at the places where the most people chant and pray: at the Yuki shrine, the main temple complex and the hall of the Amida Buddha. The gods and other beings present in a place also have a great influence on the energies perceived present on the mountain.

Some of the energies on Kurama seem to greet all comers, and are always present. Other energies are either not always present or seem to choose with whom to connect. The founder of Reiki, Mikao Usui, meditated for twenty-one days on the mountain, and it was not until the twenty-first day that he received the energy that became Reiki. The mountain seems to be home to hundreds of spiritual energies of all types and sizes. Some seem quite small, like fairy or other natural energies. Some feel very large and powerful. Some are connected to a particular location on the mountain, while some seem to wander around an area.

The Effect of the Mountain on Visitors

Many visitors just hike up and down the mountain. They may feel the energy, but for them it just seems part of why they enjoy hiking in the mountains. The more time the visitor spends on the mountain, the stronger the experience will be. Spending time connecting to the energy of the pictures in this book will help the visitor have a stronger experience when they are actually standing on the mountain.

Some visitors spend time in silent meditation, others walk the mountain and some sit and watch the world. Some visitors may become overloaded with energy, and may feel a little dizzy or even grumpy. Getting off the mountain is the best solution; however, in the meantime, sitting in an area on the mountain that is not a major energy spot, and eating or drinking something, is helpful. If the visitor has the luxury of doing so, it may be better to spend several partial days on the mountain, rather than spending a single full day.

Many visitors also report having the experiences with the mountain after they have left. They report a long term to permanent increase in the amount of healing energy in their hands, and increases in their level of psychic ability.

Sending Energy in Sacred Places

Some Western Reiki practitioners and other energy healers, if they are religious, may send healing energy to God, their guides, or angels, as a form of 'thank you' offering. Because the energy is non-physical, it seems an appropriate offering to send to a non-physical being or beings. It is always polite to be discreet about sending energy, especially if there is a language barrier. Since sending energy is not a traditional thing to do, it may not always be understood or appreciated by the people at a sacred spot. A similar example would be that some might feel uncomfortable if someone started chanting in Japanese at a Christian shrine in America, even if the act was clearly well intentioned.

I asked a noted Japanese Reiki Master if he ever offered Reiki healing energy to the gods in his family's household shrine. He seemed surprised by the question, and explained the daily ritual of placing rice, water and flowers there every morning. The idea of sending Reiki just did not make sense to him. The temples, shrines and other sacred places seem to appreciate the energy, and do not seem bothered that the offerings are not made in the traditional way. I have visited a number of Japanese homes with household shrines or altars. I try to find a few minutes during my visit to mentally say "hello," ask permission, and send a little healing energy. My experience has been that the energy coming from the shrine seems stronger and brighter afterwards, as if the offering had been welcome. I have had the same experience in most temples and shrines I have visited in Japan, and have had good results everywhere I have offered energy on Kurama Mountain.

KURAMA AND REIKI

All Reiki practitioners and teachers should consider making a pilgrimage to Kurama Mountain to give thanks to the place where this marvelous healing energy entered the world. This guidebook is intended to allow Reiki people, and others, to begin to explore and understand this sacred place. The goal of this book is to create a balance between history, legend and energy to allow the reader to understand and appreciate this mountain on a deeper level. The most important Reiki site on the mountain is Ōsugi Gongen, a site near the top of the mountain, well above the main temple complex. This is generally accepted as the place on the mountain where Mikao Usui meditated for twenty-one days.

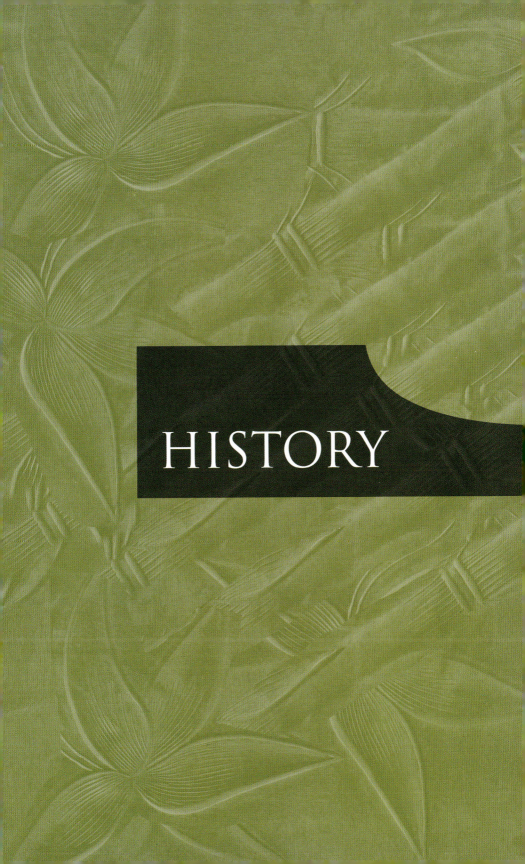

HISTORY

KURAMA THROUGH THE AGES

Kurama is not a major mountain in Japan; it is not large, nor especially well known. And yet it has a distinctive place in Japanese history and legend. After a history time line, this chapter is divided into two major sections; the first section discusses the temple in the context of Buddhism. It begins with the founding of the Kurama temple, and includes a general introduction to Japanese Buddhism and Shintoism, with a discussion of the various schools of Japanese Buddhism (and Reiki founder Mikao Usui's connection to them.)

Also included in this section are the contributions of Kurama to Japanese Buddhism with a discussion of the Kurama Kõkyõ sect that has run the Kurama Mountain temple since 1949. Information on all of the deities that appear on the mountain is included in a different section of this book.

The second section covers other aspects of historic interest about the mountain. It discusses the famous story of the Kurama Tengu and the samurai hero Yoshitsune. It includes information on Emperors and Empresses who have been to the mountain, as well as Kurama's role in various Japanese literary classics. It describes Kurama's festivals, role in martial arts, and its natural history and hazards.

Kurama Mountain is a sacred mountain due north of Japan's old imperial capital of Kyoto. In the twelve centuries of its existence, the temple complex has become a rich tapestry of legend, tradition, history and natural beauty. Emperors have meditated here. Warriors have trained here. Gods have visited. There are poisonous snakes, flowering trees and foliage, and even ancient sea fossils from the beginnings of life on the planet. There are Buddhist temples, Shinto shrines, sacred trees and sacred waters. Thousands of people come here to pray, meditate or hike.

Kurama Mountain is mentioned by name on the Usui memorial, put up a year after Mikao Usui's death.

Kurama has had the reputation for over a millennium as a spiritual-energy power spot. Reiki, one of the world's most popular forms of energy healing, began when the founder meditated for twenty-one days on this mountain back in the early 1910's or 1920's. To honor this aspect of the mountain, this book includes exercises and information about the energy of different places.

KURAMA'S HISTORICAL TIME LINE

1 A.D.   Japan is first mentioned in Chinese records as land of "Wa" (peace).

500   The founding of the Kibune Shrine on the northern side of Kurama Mountain.

538   Introduction of Buddhism to Japan from Korea. Buddhism becomes a major force by end of the century, especially with the aristocracy.

710–784 Nara is the Imperial Capital.

754   Buddhist priest, Jianzhen (Ganjin in Japanese) arrives in Japan from China.

759   Jianzhen (Ganjin in Japanese) founds Toshodaiji Temple in Nara.

770   Kurama Temple is founded by Gantei, a student of Ganjin.

788   Saicho, founder of the Tendai sect, establishes temple Enryakuji northeast of Kyoto.

794   The capital is moved to Kyoto, and the emperor sends the first torchbearers to Kurama village, originating Kurama's Fire Festival.

796   The famous Toji architect, Isendo Fujiwara, sees visions of Kannon on Kurama, and builds shrines on the mountain.

823   Kukai, founder of the Shingon sect, is appointed

abbot of Toji (in Kyoto) which becomes the headquarters of that sect.

Circa. 850 Kurama temple joins Tendai Buddhism, becoming a subtemple of Enryakuji.

938 Buddhist monk, Kuya, known for popularizing Pure Land Buddhism, begins chanting the 'Nembutsu' in Kyoto.

940 Rebellion by Taira no Masakado in Hitachi province is the first major rebellion of the warrior class against the government.

940 An oratory is moved to the Yuki shrine from the Imperial palace, to help protect the capital from the negative influences associated with the direction north.

966 *Sei Shōnagon's Pillow Book* is first published. It is still a Japanese literary classic. It mentions Kurama Mountain.

1003 A priest kills a great serpent at a well near Kurama's main temple. Its mate offers to guard the purity of the well. The Takekiri Festival is held yearly in honor of this event.

1156 Rivalry between the Taira and the Minamoto family for political power at court begins.

1160 The Taira family destroys the Minamoto family and takes power at court.

1160 The infant Yoshitsune Minamoto is brought to Kurama Temple to be raised.

1170 Yoshitsune encounters a Tengu on Kurama, and undergoes military training.

1175 Yoshitsune at sixteen years old (the age of adulthood) leaves Kurama to seek his destiny.

1180 Yoshitsune and his two surviving brothers of the Minamoto clan begin their war against the Taira family.

1185   The Minamoto clan defeats the Taira.

1189   Yoshitsune is killed by his older brother Yoritomo, who is jealous of his popularity and fears he will take over the clan.

1192   Yoritomo Minamoto (Yoshitsune's brother) is appointed by the emperor as 'seii tai' shogun (barbarian expelling generallismo), and becomes Japan's first shogun. This signals the beginning of Japan's Kamakura period.

Circa. 1200 The first annual Kurama's Nyōhō Shakyooe festival is held. This is a time when people meditate outside for three days to contemplate the nature of 'true self'.

1271   Marco Polo sets out on his journey to the court of the Mongol emperor, Kublai Khan.

1274, 1281 The Mongols twice attempt to invade Japan and are vanquished by the 'Kami kaze', or divine winds (typhoon/hurricane). This is considered "proof" of the power of the Shinto gods.

1490   Kurama temple is seven hundred years old.

1492   Christopher Columbus 'discovers' America.

1543   Matchlock muskets are first brought to Japan by the Portuguese. Tempura is one example of a 'Japanese' food that was originally introduced by the Portuguese during this period.

1548   The first Christian mission in Japan is established.

1600   The English pilot William Adams arrives in Japan. He later becomes a valued advisor to Shogun Tokugawa Ieyasu, (This historical figure is fictionalized in the popular novel, Shogun).

1614   Christianity is banned throughout Japan, condemned as a foreign influence, less drastic initial bans started in 1587.

1639   Westerners are evicted from Japan (except the Dutch, whose activities are strictly limited). Westerners are prohibited from entering Japan until the 1850's.

1707   The last eruption of Mt. Fuji (near Tokyo).

1770   Kurama Temple is 1000 years old.

1853   Commodore Perry brings a modern navy fleet (two tall ships & two steam ships) and over the next few years, forces treaties to open Japan to trade.

1865   The birth of Mikao Usui, who later founds the Reiki Healing system.

1867   The Meiji Emperor is 'restored' to power, ending the rule of the shogun in Japan.

1868   Separation of Shinto and Buddhism. Many Buddhist priests serving at Shinto shrines are forced to abandon their vows and return to the laity. This also would have occurred on Kurama Mountain.

1868   Edo is renamed "Tokyo" or Eastern Capital, and becomes the official capital the following year. Kyoto falls upon hard times.

April 1945 Kurama Temple (main temple) burns, taken as a sign about WWII.

Aug. 1945 Japan surrenders in WWII.

1949   Kurama Temple becomes the headquarters of the Kurama Kōkyō sect.

Sept 1950   The Ōsugi Gongen tree is knocked over in Hurricane Jane.

1971   The last major fire on Kurama. The main temple is rebuilt.

THE FOUNDING OF KURAMA TEMPLE
AND ITS MAJOR DEITIES

The story of the temple's founding that appears in the Mt. Kurama brochure tells the following story: "In the first year of Hoki (A.D. 770), Gantei, who was the best pupil of High Priest Ganjin, the founder of the Toshodaiji Temple in Nara, led by a white horse, climbed up to this holy place. His soul was enlightened with the realization of Bishamon-ten (the protector of the northern quarter of the Buddhist heaven and the spirit of the sun). Following, he founded the Buddhist temple on Mt. Kurama. Later, in the 15th year of Enryaku (AD 796), the chief officer in charge of the construction of Toji Temple saw a vision of Senju-kannon (The thousand-armed Kannon and the spirit of the moon) and built temples and pagodas on the mountain. Further research into the history of the temple has verified the essential details of the story.

Buddhism was first introduced to Japan from Korea around 538 A.D. It took nearly a thousand years to migrate from India, its place of origin. Over successive centuries, Japan sent to China for Buddhist priests, to teach and refine Buddhist doctrine.

The "High Priest Ganjin" is a famous Chinese historical figure during this period. As a Chinese priest, Ganjin was invited by the Japanese Emperor to ordain priests and legitimize Japanese Buddhism in the eyes of the Buddhist world. Ganjin's Chinese name was Jian Zhen, also spelled Chien Chen. He tried to reach Japan five times, during which time he became blind. He finally arrived in Japan in 754, and after five years of work, he was granted an imperial decree to build the renowned Toshodaiji temple in Nara.

There are three documents which discuss the founding of Kurama Temple written between 1150 and 1712.[20] The stories vary slightly and while all mention that Bishamonten was the original deity of the mountain, only one of the accounts mentions Gantei as founding the temple in 770. The others focus more on the rebuilding and expansion of the temple by the famous architect Fujiwara Isendo (some sources say Ishito).

All three stories emphasize that Fujiwara originally intended to build a shrine to Kannon, and when he was divinely led to the mountain (by horse and by dream), that he discovered Bishamonten (Sanskrit name Vaishravana). This confused him, until he had a dream that Bishamonten and Kannon (Kwan Yin) were somehow two facets of the same being. The modern addition of Maõ-son to be a third facet of the same being the people of Kurama Temple call Sonten seems a logical progression.

Ganjin's student, Gantei,[21] had two visions which led to the founding of Kurama Temple. In the first vision, he was told to leave Nara and search for a sacred mountain near to what later became Kyoto. He had his second vision while he was on his journey. In this vision, he saw a white horse with a saddle, which held treasure, a traditional reference to the white horse that carried the Buddhist Sutras. When he awoke and looked around, he saw the twin-peaks of Kurama Mountain and the saddle between them, and he knew he had been guided there. The name "kurama" comes from combining the words 'kura', which means horse saddle, and 'yama', which means mountain. Even in the eighth century, Kurama had the reputation of being a powerful energy spot. After having been led to the mountain, Gantei meditated and "...his soul was enlightened with the realization of Bishamonten." Another account of Gantei's vision describes how he was attacked by a she-demon and rescued by Bishamonten at the hour of the tiger on the day of the tiger, in the month of the tiger, which is on the first day of the new year.

In the *Lotus Sutra*, Bishamonten is the guardian of the northern quadrant of Buddhist heaven. He has vowed to protect the Buddha from harm. In gratitude for his rescue, Gantei founded Kurama Temple, dedicating it to the god Bishamonten.

Gantei may have been inspired in part to build a temple to Bishamonten in 770 because of an event related to Bishamonten that happened 4 years prior in the then imperial capital of Nara. Since his teacher Ganjin was in Nara, Gantei might well have participated in these events. The imperially-sanctioned history Shoku Nihongi, written in the early Heian period [Heian period 884-1185], notes that in the 10th month of 766, a relic appeared from the body of the Bishamonten statue in Sumidera temple (now Kairyuoh-ji in Nara). Several hundred people of rank carried the relic in a procession around the city. An imperial order was issued to officials to worship the relic.[22]

Kurama Temple is actually a little older than Kyoto,

which was founded in 794. It is interesting that the temple is due north of Kyoto's imperial palace, as it seems logical for Kurama to be the northern guardian of Kyoto, since Bishamonten guarded the north side of the Buddha. However, there are no records indicating that the location of Kurama Temple played a role in exactly where the imperial palace was located, and thus where Kyoto was located.

By the end of the tenth century Kurama Temple was one of the most widely known and visited Kannon temples in the Kyoto/Osaka area. Other popular Kannon sites of this time were Ishiyama, Kiyomizudera, Hasedera, Tsubosakadera and Kokawadera. Other temples were added to this group in the eleventh and twelfth centuries to make a total of thirty-three.

There are several stories as to how Maō-son, a deity unique to the Kurama Temple, became associated with Kurama Mountain. In one legend, told by the famous Kuki family, Maō-son appeared when a meteorite landed from the planet Venus. A piece of this meteorite is now enshrined on Kurama Mountain.[23]

Another story refers to the vision of a warrior god from Venus descending to earth in a fiery chariot six–million years ago. He landed at a spot called "Okunoin." Maō-son is thought to be a guardian and guide for both the physical and the spiritual evolution of mankind. He is seen as the conqueror of evil, whose mission is the salvation of mankind and all living things.[24] All three of Kurama's deities, Bishamonten, Maō-son and Kannon are emanations from the divine Source called Sonten. This title translates as "Respectable Heaven," or "Honorable Universe." While Sonten has been at the temple since its beginning, it was not until the Kōkyō sect took over Kurama Temple in 1949 that Sonten became the dominant deity of the temple.

The headquarters of Tendai Buddhism was located on near-by Mt. Hiei, (founded in 788 A.D) and Kurama Temple became a Tendai sub-temple. It remained part of the Tendai sect until Kurama Temple broke away after WWII. Kurama Kōkyō Buddhism continues to include with different emphasis the traditional Tendai deities of the Amida Buddha, Bishamonten, Fudō-myo, and the Bodhisatvas Kannon (Kwan Yin) and Jizō.. Kurama Kōkyō took over Kurama in 1948. The post-WWII period in Japan led many to decide that Japan must become new, and Kurama Temple, like many temples all over Japan, broke away from their parent sects and formed its own sect.

BUDDHISM AND SHINTO

Buddhism and Shinto are the two major religions in Japan. Many spiritual places in Japan such as Kurama Mountain are a combination of Buddhist and Shinto structures. The structure can be identified as being Buddhist or Shinto based on what it is called. If a building is called a temple it is Buddhist, if it called a shrine it is Shinto. This designation has nothing to do with the size or shape of the building.

HOW TO RECOGNIZE A SHINTO SHRINE

Shinto Shrines are typically outdoors, with a torii somewhere near the site. The torii is the major symbol of Shinto. The torii consists of two vertical pillars, and two crossbeams. They are usually made of stone or red-painted wood. The torii comes from the legend of the Sun goddess, Amatserasu who had locked her self away in a cave, depriving the world of Light. The word 'torii' means 'bird perch,' and this was the structure from which the rooster crowed to announce the entertainment the gods had planned, to lure Amatserasu from her cave.

Shinto

Shinto is the native religion of Japan. The term Shinto did not appear until the late sixth or early seventh century, after the introduction of Buddhism required the native religion to have a name. Shinto is not a cohesive religion at all, though various efforts over the centuries have tried to codify it, with limited success. Shinto is divided into the Great and Little traditions, which relate to different areas of life. Both are described here, but only Little tradition Shinto appears on Kurama.

The Great Tradition Shinto

While Great Tradition Shinto does not appear on Kurama, it is mentioned here because of its impact on Twentieth Century history. The Great Tradition of Shinto concerns the Emperor, and his history as the living descendent of an unbroken chain of emperors, originating from the offspring of the great sun goddess, Amatserasu Omikami. Japan's sense of itself as a divine land under a divine ruler came from this legend. The Great Tradition of Shinto was used by the state starting in the Meiji restoration (1868-1912), to unify Japan under the divine rule of the Emperor, as both spiritual and worldly leader. Great tradition Shinto's hold on Japan was broken after World War II when the defeated emperor was forced to renounce his divinity. Great Tradition Shinto is still a hot topic in a Japan trying to distance itself from the State Shinto of its past. On May 15, 2000, the Prime Minister Yoshiro Mori made a statement in which he used the phrase. "Tenno o chushin to suru kami no kuni," [the nation with the Emperor at its heart in the land of deities]. There was such a firestorm of protest he was forced to call a press conference to formally apologize for his remark. Outrage was so strong that the Prime Minister and his party nearly lost the subsequent election.

The Little Tradition of Shinto

The Little Tradition of Shinto refers to all other aspects of this religion that are not part of the Great Tradition. The little tradition of Shinto is visible in numerous places on Kurama. Shinto Little Tradition includes Nature worship, polytheism and shamanism, ancestor worship, and agricultureal and fertility rites.

Shinto derives from the people's faith and practices that are handed-down over time. There is no unifying structure or theology in Shinto. Many rituals and deities are connected to particular locales. In designating what is worthy of worship, Shinto makes no sharp distinctions between kami (gods) and people. Anything that is excellent, awe-inspiring, impressive or striking can be a kami. This can include heroes, emperors, rocks, streams, mountains and buildings. The goal of Shinto is to provide one with appreciation, and a sense of awe in the face of the mysteries of life. Shinto believes that nature is intrinsically good, beautiful and valuable for itself. This belief has strongly influenced much of Japanese art and culture.

On Kurama there are a wide variety of kami. A number of very large trees are considered to be kami, as well as springs, and even the stone cover of the crypt which once housed the sacred writings. Kami are considered to be typically good, requiring only proper attention and respect as shown by prayers and offerings of rice, sake or other food items, and even money. Prayers ask the kami to grant petitions (often for good luck or success), and thank the kami for the blessings they have bestowed. Shinto deities are not typically anthropomorphic; (i.e. they are not thought to have a visible form apart from the physical appearance of the place the kami dwells). There are numerous kami all over Kurama, indicated by spirit ropes. Spirit ropes indicate what areas are sacred. The spirit rope has dangling rope tassels and folded paper thunderbolts. Offerings of sake and coins are often left at kami sites.

Purification is an essential element of Shinto. Outer purification is symbolized by rinsing the hands and the mouth at the purification shrines. Inner purification is achieved through prayer and meditation. Disease, bleeding and wrongdoing are considered to be pollutants which must be cleansed to restore harmony. This emphasis is visible in Japan's focus on bathing, and on using purification salt before sumo wrestling matches and after funerals. There are a number of purification basins on Kurama, some are a simple puddle, formed by a spring, and others are elaborate, roofed structures.

Japanese Schools of Buddhism

Like many foreigners unfamiliar with Buddhism, I once thought Buddhism was relatively simple. It consisted of the Buddha, who wasn't really a god, but a man who reached enlightenment, and that was it. Buddhism in Japan is anything but simple. It has evolved out of Mahayana Buddhism and includes many deities from India where Buddhism began, but also includes Hindu deities such as Sarasvati, and has been heavily influenced by Tibetan, Korean and especially Chinese Buddhism.

Because of Kyoto's prominence as the capital of Japan for twelve centuries, many forms of Japanese Buddhism that are important today developed there. (A number of schools of Buddhism developed even earlier when Nara was the capital, and are called Nara Buddhism.) The three main groups of Japanese Buddhist schools are the Esoteric schools, the "quick path" schools such as Jodo, and the Zen schools. The esoteric Buddhist sects are Shingon and Tendai. Both are fairly eclectic, and include ascetic rituals for attaining spiritual or magical power. These rituals often include fasting, meditation and pilgrimage hikes.

Kurama Mountain was part of Tendai Buddhism for most of its twelve centuries. Tendai Buddhism focuses on the book *The Lotus Sutra* as its main text. Its primary deities are Bishamonten, Kannon and Fudō Myo, which are considered to be aspects of Amida Buddha. Most popular of the "quick path" schools is Jodo. The name Jodo translates to "Pure Land" Buddhism. It emphasized the average person could achieve enlightenment easily in the next life. All one needed to do was pray with sincerity to the Amida Buddha, and one would be reborn into the "Pure Land" Once in the pure land which was free from worldly distractions, enlightenment would be much easier to obtain. The Jodo sect believes that one must repeat the mantra many times. Jodo Shinshu sect believes it must be said with sincerity only once. The mantra is called the "nembutsu." The mantra is the syllables "Namu Amida Butsu" which translates as "Homage to Amida Buddha." Another similar form of Kyoto Japanese Buddhism is Nichiren, though it focuses on a different mantra from *The Lotus Sutra* and is more strict.

Zen Buddhism originated in China. There were four schools of Zen in Japan. The most popular are Rinzai and Soto, both of which focus on meditation practice. In Rinzai, students are given Zen sayings called koans to contemplate. The most well known koan outside Japan is "What is the sound of one hand clapping?" Practitioners sit in a room and all face the same direction, so that if anyone moves, all notice it. In Soto Buddhism there are no koans, and practitioners face the wall when meditating. The Obaku school is the smallest and is known for their calligraphy. The Fuke sect played the bamboo flute as its meditation practice. Fuke's popularity among potentially rebellious samurai during the Edo period led to it being banned in 1871 as part of the Meiji era's abolishment of the institutions of shogun and samurai.

THE ORIGIN OF BUDDHISM

Central to Buddhism is the original, historical Buddha who lived about 500 B.C. Siddhartha Gautama achieved enlightenment at age 35, and spent the rest of his life teaching others about it. He did not consider himself to be a god or a follower of any god. Buddhism focuses on living a moral life, being aware of one's thoughts and actions, and developing wisdom and understanding.[25] Buddhism changed as it crossed Asia, picking up some of the character of the religions of the countries it passed through. One of the most startling additions, to most westerners, is the existence of Buddhist gods. As Buddhism intermingled with different cultures, other beings were added to the pantheon and other ideas were introduced.

Japanese Buddhism is a form of Mahayana Buddhism. Mahayana Buddhism focuses on not only the historical Buddha, but other Buddhas and Bodhisatvas as well. This form of Buddhism was carried along the northern routes of Tibet, China, Taiwan, Japan, Korea, Mongolia, and then into parts of Southeast Asia.

THE CHANGING FATES OF BUDDHISM AND SHINTO

Buddhism was introduced into Japan from Korea in 552 A.D. It sparked an intense period of cultural borrowing, which lasted until the middle of the ninth century. Buddhist temples inspired Shinto to create shrines. Buddhism's emphasis on the world as a place where one's goal is to be released from the cycle of death and rebirth is in sharp contrast to Shinto's celebration of life. Buddhism quickly came into prominence over the next five-hundred years as it was strongly embraced by the imperial family, and thus by the nobles.

Kurama Mountain was founded in 770 A.D., when Buddhism was increasing in influence. From 1185 to 1573, a new movement declared the Shinto deities to be stronger than the Buddhist gods. The strength of the Shinto gods was shown in the late thirteenth century when kamikaze (translation 'divine wind'), typhoons destroyed a large Mongol invasion fleet, preventing it from reaching a largely undefended Japan. The Kamikaze pilots of World War II were named in honor of these protective winds that saved Japan from invasion.

For many centuries Shinto and Buddhism were practiced side-by-side. Typically each Buddhist temple had a shrine on its grounds, and each Shinto shrine similarly had a Buddhist temple on its grounds. In remote areas, a Shinto priest might even perform Buddhist ceremonies. At the beginning of the Meiji era, from the mid-to-late 1800's, Japan did its best to modernize. Even during this transformation, keeping Japan's identity was very important. Shinto was modified by the state to focus more on the Great Tradition of Shinto, of treating the emperor as the divine ruler of the country. Shinto became the state religion of Japan. Buddhism was downgraded in importance, and many temples were disbanded.

After World War II, the Emperor had to renounce his claim

to divinity. Shinto became discredited as the tool that the state had used to justify its governance. Buddhism is now much greater in importance. Shinto, at least the Little Tradition Shinto, seems to be enjoying a mild resurgence however, as modern Japanese try to reconnect to their roots.

TRADITION VS. SACRED

The Japanese are a very odd blend of secular and sacred. The shifting fates of Buddhism and Shinto have led to an odd sort of ambivalence about religion in the culture. Most Japanese do not consider themselves to be religious, yet many of these same people visit shrines and temples as a leisure activity. They visit family graves on the correct days, several times a year. They buy charms and will say a few prayers, and throw coins in the offering box, simply because this is what people do at these places.

Most of the older homes have household shrines and altars. People still place offerings at these shrines every day or at least on holidays. Many claim that is not religious, merely traditional.

MORE ON BUDDHISM AND KURAMA

Gantei, who founded Kurama Temple, was a student of Ganjin. Ganjin founded the Ritsu sect of Buddhism with the building of Toshodaiji Temple in Nara (Nara was the capital of Japan.) In the third year of the Tenpyo Hoji Era (A.D. 759) Ganjin was invited to Japan from T'ang Dynasty, China by the Japanese Emperor Shomu. Ganjin finally succeeded in visiting Japan in A.D. 754 in his sixth attempt. [26]

The temple later converted to Tendai, probably in the first one hundred years after its founding. Temple affiliations were fairly fluid at this time, as Buddhism was still getting established. The temple remained a Tendai temple under the Tendai headquarters in nearby Enryakuji temple on Mt. Hiei, until the mountain split off to form its own sect in 1949.

Pure Land Buddhism

Buddhism gained new following among the common folk with the arrival of Pure Land Buddhism. To be reborn into Amida's paradise, one must only recite with sincerity the "Nembutsu" phrase, "All praise to the Amida Buddha." The Buddhist priest, Ryounin (1037–1132 A.D) first articulated this idea. In 1095, while a priest at Mt Hiei, he retired to a hermitage to study the sutras. In 1117, while he was meditating, the Amida Buddha appeared to him, and gave him the message that by reciting the Nembutsu benefits accrue to both oneself and all of one's ancestors.

Kurama Mountain comes into the story in 1124, when Ryounin meditates there and receives a message from Bishamonten that he is to spread this revelation to others. He spent the next nine years traveling and preaching in Kyoto and around Japan. This story was described, on a no longer existing scroll, called The History and Benefits of Yuuzuu Nenbutsu. This was first written in 1314, and illustrated soon after. Copies of the scroll (still existing) were used to encourage donations, and to solidify the network of affiliated temples.[27]

Yamabushi – Shaman priests

Kurama has long been connected to Shinto and shamanic practices. Yamabushi practice a combination of Buddhist and Shinto esoteric rituals with the goal of achieving supernatural powers. Some of these rituals include standing for hours beneath a waterfall in winter, making pilgrimages circumambulating sacred mountains, meditating and fasting in the wilderness. The stories of the Yamabushi and the Tengu have often melded together as in the following description:

"On an afternoon in November 1963, I went to Kurama temple with the intention of walking over the top of the mountain and down the other side to Kibune. A little way down from the summit, I heard from among the trees a strong hard voice reciting what sounded like mantras. I left the path and followed the voice, until in a clearing in a forest I saw an enormous cryptomeria tree, its huge trunk girdled about with the belt of straw rope, and before it, with her back to me, a woman seated on the ground reciting.

The hard-base voice continued for several minutes, through a number of invocations which were unfamiliar to me, while the woman sat perfectly motionless with a long rosary in her hands. Suddenly I heard some words I understood. Over and over again she called upon the daitengu and the shotengu -- the large tengu and the small tengu -- at the end of her invocation turning towards the forest and clapping her hands. Venturing to approach her, I asked if there were still a good many tengu to be found on the mountain. She turned to face me, a brown face peculiarly like an old bird, with an expression fierce yet remote and a pair of extraordinarily glittering eyes." [28]

KURAMA KŌKYŌ BUDDHISM

World War II shook the faith of many Japanese in the value of the old ways and traditions. As they began to build a new Japan, many young people felt the need to create new institutions. Kurama Kōkyō broke away from the Tendai Buddhist sect in 1949 to form their own Buddhist sect. While Kurama Kōkyō has their own system of beliefs, they consider themselves stewards of the mountain, and welcome visitors of all backgrounds and philosophies. Everyone is invited to connect to the energy of the mountain.

Quoting from a book of Kurama's philosophy: "The energy and understanding of Sonten that people have received on Kurama has led some people to start new religions, both recently and during early times. Others founded big enterprises... Without knowing they are doing so, many people come to Kurama for a pilgrimage and are given the energy. From Kurama Mountain this wonderful power is radiated and you should take this power without hesitation." Kurama Kōkyō welcomes others to connect to the mountain their own way, but remain focused on their own religion and philosophy. Kurama temple's religion is based on Sonten, the divine force behind the cosmos. Sonten is seen as the being made up of a trinity of three of the deities that have been part of Kurama Mountain since its beginning; Maō-son, Bishamonten and Kannon.

In Arjava Petter's Reiki Dharma Newsletter #14, he describes the temple philosophy of living. "The Kurama temples suggests three rules of conduct: 1) Do not talk badly about others, and do not do anything unethical. Work on yourself! 2) Be honest and work for the good of humanity. 3) Immerse yourself in the Universal Life Force and trust it unconditionally. Then it will carry you."[29]

KURAMA KŌKYŌ TEMPLE FOUNDER

To the left of the Amida Buddha statue, in a small alcove, is a statue of the founder of the Kurama Kōkyō sect, Kooun Shigaraki. The Kurama Kōkyō sect has run Kurama temple since 1949, and considers itself stewards of the mountain. His daughter, Konin Shigaraki is Kurama's current abbess. She took over after his death in 1972 and is now eighty-years-old.

KURAMA'S MOST FAMOUS LEGENDS:
Kurama Tengu and Yoshitsune

The most famous legend about Kurama is the story of how the twelfth-century samurai hero, Yoshitsune (Yo-she-sue-nay), was trained in the martial arts by the mythic, goblin-like Tengu on Kurama Mountain. This tale is the subject of numerous Noh plays and children stories. It inspired an early Japanese movie, a postage stamp and even a tengu-brand of Japanese beef jerky.

THE TENGU

The Kurama tengu are a race of human-like creatures with red faces and long noses. They are considered to be oni, which are Japanese goblins or demons. The Kurama tengu were famed for being highly proficient in martial arts, and the arts of war. There are other kinds of tengu in Japanese literature, but the Kurama tengu are considered to be the

 most powerful. Tengu are portrayed as being more mischievous than evil and are often depicted as helping people.[30] Symbols of Kurama tengu are everywhere on Kurama. Tengu key chains are

favorite souvenirs, as are tengu masks. The temple's crest is sometimes seen as a stylized tengu fan, although elsewhere it is described as a chrysanthemum seen from the side. Who were the Karuma tengu that taught the samurai Yoshitsune? The Kurama tengu might have been esoteric priests called Yamabushi, whose ascetic practices in the mountains gained them magical powers. Or possibly, they were a band of military monks on Kurama and took the name Kurama Tengu to increase their fame. Another theory is that the Kurama Tengu were really shipwrecked Russians who made their way into the mountains. The red skin is explained by the heat and humidity of the Japanese summer. Even today, Japanese children and college students will often draw their Caucasian friends as having extraordinarily large noses.

Painted Illustration of Kurama and Crow beaked Tengu (date unknown - author's collection)

YOSHITSUNE (1159-1189)

Samurai and martial arts fans come to Kurama Mountain to see where the legendary samurai hero, Yoshitsune, lived, slept, drunk water, practiced swordsmanship, and even measured his height before leaving the mountain to seek his destiny. The story of Yoshitsune is one of the most famous samurai stories in Japan, and is featured in numerous Noh plays, folk tales, paintings, and television show. Yoshitsune grew up and was trained in martial arts on Kurama, before he left to raise an army to defeat the clan that had destroyed his father and family. Yoshitsune's boyhood name was Ushiwaka-maru.

YOSHITSUNE'S STORY:

In the twelfth century the emperor and aristocracy had little power; instead, two samurai houses struggled against each other for influence. The Heike clan decisively won over the Genji clan in 1159. The head of the Genji clan was betrayed and killed; the eldest son, Yoritomo, imprisoned. Yoshitsune, the youngest son, still a baby, was not killed but given to Kurama Temple to become a Buddhist monk. The head of the triumphant Heike clan became regent to the emperor and his rule was harsh.

Yoshitsune grew up at Kurama Temple, however, he was not content with just learning Buddhist scriptures. According to legend, the head of the Kurama Tengu came to the young Yoshitsune, and revealed to the orphan that he was really a son of the Genji clan. The 'King of the Kurama Tengu' taught him military strategy, tactics and swordsmanship.

Another version of the story is that Yoshitsune's teacher

was Kiichi Hogen who wrote various works on military tactics and strategy. Others say that Yoshitsune only read his works. There is also an allusion to a famous fortune teller to the government named Seimei Abeno who used a means of divination called Onmyo-ji, which translates to "yin yang master." There is a very famous shrine to this fortune teller, aristocrat and reputedly magic maker on Horikawa Street, in Kyoto.[31]

A third version of the story states that there is a monument in Kibune at the site of Kiichi Hogen's house, which confirms that Kiichi Hogen taught Yoshitsune military tactics. This story also adds a touch of romantic tragedy, as it is said that: "Hogen's daughter Jorurihime fell in love with Yoshitsune, but Yoshitsune stole a secret document about military tactics possessed by Hogen. Hogen discovered the theft and tried to kill Yoshitsune, but he himself was killed in the attempt. Lovelorn Jorurihime later committed suicide."[32]

Be it man or Tengu, whoever taught Yoshitsune martial arts taught him well. History credits him with both a mastery

of martial arts and the ability to lead large forces in battle. Yoshitsune gathered the remnants of the Genji clan and created an army to fight against the Heike clan. His oldest brother, Yoritomo, escaped from prison and raised his own army. The armies were kept separate, and both were formidable fighting forces, though Yoshitsune's army was the most successful. Over the next few years (1180-1185) Yoshitsune successfully won several battles and finally defeated the Heike, putting the Genji clan in control.

Yoshitsune was hailed a great hero, and many thought he should be the ruler of Japan. The eldest brother, Yoritomo, was the head of the Genji clan, and he was jealous of his brother's fame. Yoritomo accused his hero brother of being a traitor and ordered him to be slain. While historians believe he was indeed slain, some legends say he escaped to Mongolia where he became the warrior Genghis Khan. After Yoshitsune's death (or exile), Yoritomo became the first Shogun of Japan, beginning the Kamakura Shogunate period (1192-1333).

MARTIAL ARTS AND KURAMA

The story of Yoshitsune is a wellspring for Japanese martial arts. This 12th century hero was famed for both his military successes leading armies and his success in hand to hand combat. Yoshitsune-ryu no longer exists as a separate style, but was incorporated into other martial arts styles through the ages, most notably Ninpo/Ninjustsu. Practitioners of this are more commonly known as Ninjas. *(Pg. 35, Adams)* Ninpo/ Ninjutsu emphasizes infiltration into hostile enemy territory; modern practitioners use both armed and unarmed fighting techniques, hidden weapons, sword evasion, hiding, and special body conditioning. The Samurai hero Yoshitsune was one of the greatest fighters and generals of his age, and he was well taught in martial arts while he lived on Kurama Mountain. Some of these teachings have survived in various families historically connected to Kurama Mountain, most especially the Kuki family. The Kuki family are said to have preserved the teachings of Yoshitsune's teacher, Kiichi (Alternately Kiitsu) Hogen, and also to have preserved other Shinto teachings.

These teachings have been included in the martial arts taught by the Kuki family, and incorporated over the centuries into various martial arts styles. Aikido is the best known style to incorporate at least some elements of this teaching. Other martial arts describing a connection to the Kuki family's teaching are Tenshinhyoho, and the style taught by the Kuki family called Kuki Shin Ryu (alternately spelled Kuki Shinden Ryu). Kuki Shin Ryu is a battlefield oriented martial art which includes unarmed fighting, and a number of weapon techniques including bo staff, sword and projectiles. Techniques are done assuming the combatants are wearing armor. A Kuki family legend also tells of a meteorite from the planet Venus which broke into three pieces, one of which is enshrined at Okunoin. *(See Deities: Maõ-son essay)* The name "Kuki" was given to the family by the emperor in the 14th century, because the Samurai Yakushimaru Takazane (alternately spelled Yasushimaru Takazaneu) who fought for the emperor was said to have fought like Kuki which translates as "nine demons."

Kurama Mountain also has had a tradition of sword smithing. In the year 1492 one of the Heianjo swordsmiths of the Yamashiro schools set up a workshop at the gate of Kurama Temple at the end of the Onin war. Ninpo/Ninjutsu also claims the Kurama Tengu legend. "Winged Long Nosed Goblins called Tengu are the legendary, original ninja from whom all Ninja are said to have sprung." *Kiichi* [33] Hogen is said to have taught the martial arts to the famous twelfth-century general and strategist Minamoto no Yoshitsune, but he imparted the truly secret skills of the sword only to the "Eight Priests of Kurama," and it was with these that the Eight Schools began. [Kurama Hachi Ryu] Hogen was famous for his strategy. "[34]Martial arts can be powerful both in defending authority and in refuting it. "

At the end of the period in 1185 the central government in Kyoto was so weak that it was ruled at night by three robbers who had learned Ninjitsu from the yamabushi of Mt. Kurama, north of the capital." [35]The great Samurai Miyamoto Musashi [~1584-1645] used two swords, one long and one short. His biographer claims this is because his father and adoptive father were swordsmen, but he practiced different styles and could not decide between them, so began wielding both. His adoptive father used the Kurama-ryu style with a 27-inch sword.[36] Miyamoto Musashi's *Book of Five Rings*, is still in print.

Another sixteenth century martial artist claimed to have received divine revelation on Mt. Kurama, which led to the creation of his style. "Jion of the Nen-ryu was enlightened to the secrets of his style at Kurama Temple in Kyoto"[37] Some of the teachings of Kiichi Hogen have survived in the archives of the Kuki family, which has been long connected with Kurama Mountain. These teachings have been incorporated over the centuries into various martial arts styles. Aikido is the best known style to incorporate some of the elements of this teaching. Other martial arts styles that have a connection to the Kuki family teachings are Tenshinhyoho[38] and Kuki Shin Ryu.[39]

The founder of Aikido, Morihei Ueshiba (1883-1969), also studied with the Kuki family (along with training with many other teachers) He retreated to the Kurama area a number of times during the 1920s. He is known to have studied weapon styles here.[40] In Aikido, most of the techniques that do not involve bending or manipulation of joints are known as Kōkyō-ho and are breath or timing techniques. [41] "Like the concept of Ki, Kōkyō can take on broad cosmological significance or meta-physical significance. One can portray divine reality as literally breathing all things into existence and giving them life. A person imitates this cosmic phenomenon in the recitation of *kotodama*, sacred words (actually syllables) that in Shinto belief hold the key to the secrets of divine creation. Ueshiba was extensively trained and deeply committed to this practice." [42] This concept of breath as divinity also connects to the name of the sect that runs Kurama Temple in the present, Kurama Kōkyō.

The Kuki martial arts family is connected to Kurama Mountain in another way. According to an ancient legend in the family, a meteorite from Venus fell onto Japan and broke into three pieces. All three fragments were found and enshrined in various temples. The one that fell on or near Kurama was later enshrined in Okunoin as "Maõ-son." [43]

MURASAKI SHIKIBU

Kurama is also the backdrop for several scenes in *The Tale of Genji*, another Japanese literary classic. The authoress was one of Sei Shōnagon's contemporaries and rivals at court. Between them they painted a vivid picture of court life of the period.

SARASHINA NIKKI

Another famous book of the same period is *Sarashina's Diary* (recently titled, *As I Crossed the Bridge of Dreams* written by Sarashina Nikki also in the eleventh century). She describes her trip to Kurama very poetically... "In the spring I went to Kurama Temple. It was a soft spring day, with mist trailing over the mountain. The mountain people brought tokoro [a kind of root] as the only food and I found it good. In God's absent month I went again, and the mountain views along the way were more beautiful than before, the mountain-side brocaded with the autumn colors. The stream, rushing headlong, boiled-up like molten metal and then shattered into crystals. When I reached the monastery, the maple leaves, wet with a shower, were brilliant beyond compare. The pattern of the maple leaves in autumn dyed with the rain... beautiful in the deep mountain!" -Sarashina Nikki

AKIKO AND TEKKAN YOSANO

Contemporary poets associated with Kurama Temple are Akiko Yosano (1868-1942) and her husband Tekkan(1868-1942). The Yosanos came to Kurama on a number of occasions and wrote several poems about the mountain. Akiko's study was donated to the temple after her death. The study is the small building just outside Kurama Temple's museum. Some poetry manuscripts and personal effects are also on display in the Yosano Memorial Room, on the second floor of the museum.

Akiko Yosano was a feminist. She was also a radical, a social critic and a poet. She fell in love with, and openly lived with Tekkan Yosano, a married man and magazine publisher. They eventually married, and had a dozen children. As a pacifist, she spoke out against the Sino-Japanese war and the growing nationalistic fervor of the times. She founded the women's college, the Bunka Gakuin. She wrote more than seventy-five books. Yosano Akiko was a pioneer-feminist, and courageously questioned even the role of the Emperor:

> *Never let them kill you, brother!*
> *His Imperial Majesty would not come out to fight...*
> *How could He possibly make them believe*
> *that it is honorable to die?*

Akiko and Tekkan wrote the following poems during one of their visits to Kurama Mountain. The following is a rough translation:

> *Good space to pray for the real world,*
> *Thanks for Rei, God*
> *Enjoy to study*
> *- Akiko*
> *This walking through the winding wood*
> *Coming up to Kurama mountain*
> *temple is good*
> *So now can get a sprinkling of soul. —* [44]*Tekkan*

Deborah Boliver Boehm

Kurama Mountain is mentioned in the 1996 memoir *A Zen Romance: One Woman's Adventures in a Monastery* by Deborah Boliver Boehm. "Kuramayama, one of Japan's most magical small mountains, [is the] legendary home of the long-nosed, red-faced goblins known as tengu. Kurama was one of my favorite haunts, the melding of natural beauty (deep woods, celestial vistas) with complex mythology (snake-woman, tiger-gods, flying pyromaniacs) always left me feeling exalted and inspired." Snake woman refers to the snake spirit who guards the well at the main temple, the Akai-gohō-zenjin Shrine. Tiger gods probably refers to the tiger guardians of the temple. Flying pyromaniacs refers to Maõ-son's arrival on earth in a fiery chariot.

ANIME AND MANGA

A different meaning of the word Rei-ki appears in numerous Japanese anime and manga. The word Rei, is much like the word spirit in English in that it can mean very different things in different contexts. The English word spirit can mean spiritual, ghost or alcohol. Reiki practitioners use the word "Rei/spirit" to mean the divine guiding spirit of the universe. In anime and manga, the word Rei/Spirit refers to the innate supernatural energy that magical and supernatural beings often use to fight with.

KURAMA FESTIVALS

The following nine festivals are mentioned in the English language version of the Karuma Mountain brochure. Some are held throughout Japan, some are particular to the mountain.

HATSUTORA FESTIVAL (ALSO KNOWN AS HATSU TORA TAISAI)

This is Japan's traditional New Year's festival. During this five-day period, people go to the temples to pray for prosperity, happiness, and the realization of their dreams. This festival is of particular interest to Kurama because it was on the first day of this festival that the temple was first founded in the year 770. The founder Gantei while meditating on Kurama had a vision of being attacked by a she-demon, and rescued by Bishamonten, which led him to build a temple to Bishamonten. Since this vision occurred at the hour of the tiger, on the day of the tiger and the month of the tiger, Kurama's temple guardians are tigers.

Setsubun (February 3)

This 'exorcism' ceremony has been performed at the imperial palace since Kyoto was founded, and is now practiced in homes and temples, all over Japan. Its purpose is to expel bad luck and evil demons, and to purify one for the coming planting season and year. The doors and windows of the homes are thrown open and toasted soybeans are tossed into the air while saying "fortune in and demons out" ("oni wa soto, fuku wa uchi, "). Another ritual involves throwing the toasted soy beans onto a clean part of the floor, then family members pick up and eat one soybean for each year of their age to ensure health and luck in the coming year.

Hana Kuyõ (mid April)

Purification ceremonies are held to honor Bishamonten, the temple's protecting deity. Offerings of flowers are given to him in appreciation for the abundance of flora and fauna on Kurama.

Uesaku Festival (full moon of May)

This festival is described in the Kurama brochure as "A mysterious festival with an international flavor celebrating the protector deity" (Bishamonten). Ue-May, Saku means full moon. Buddhists all over the world also celebrate this full moon, as the holiday Wesak. It commemorates the birth of the historical Buddha, his reaching enlightenment, and his physical death.

Takekiri Ceremony (June 20)

This ceremony is connected to one of the legends of Kurama. The story takes place at the Akai-gohõ-zenjin Shrine next to the main temple. A priest killed the giant snake that guarded the well. The snake's mate agreed to protect the water in exchange for its own life. In modern times, two groups of priests compete in cutting up large bamboo poles, which represent the snakes.

Nyohō Shakyō (August 1-3)

This is a traditional observance that has been held annually for over eight hundred years. Individuals sit among the singing birds and cool breezes while contemplating the origin of the 'true self.'

Yoshitsune Festival (September 15)

This festival commemorates Yoshitsune. Young Kendo students test their skill in dedicatory matches. Yoshitsune was one of Japan's most honored samurai warriors, whose legend said he was trained by the mythical Kurama Tengu. The festival consists of a memorial prayer service honoring Yoshitsune, followed by a display of swordsmanship.

Great Autumn Festival (October 14)

This festival commemorates the establishment of the Kurama Kōkyō sect as an independent sect of Buddhism in 1949.

Fire Festival of Kurama (October 22)

The best-known festival on Kurama Mountain is the Kurama Fire Festival. In this evening festival, the men of Kurama village carry torches and portable shrines through the streets. The torches are carried to guide the spirits of hell through the human realms. This festival began when the Emperor first began the annual tradition of sending torch-bearers to the village, back in 794.

Kurama Mountain's Natural History and Hazards

Volcanoes and Oceans

Kurama Mountain and the other mountains in this part of Japan are extinct volcanoes. Up until about fifty-five-million years ago this area was a shallow, ancient, seabed alive with trilobites, corals and other Cambrian-era creatures. The volcano that became Kurama Mountain lifted and broke through the crust in such a way that the oldest rocks, the remnants of the seabed, are at the lower elevations of the mountain, while the younger volcanic rock is at the top.

Climate

Kurama Mountain has a four season temperate climate. The most beautiful time to come is fall (mid November) when thousands of people come to the Kyoto area to see the brilliant fall foliage. It can snow on Kurama Mountain during the winter, but rarely enough to prevent hiking. Spring occurs in March and April. The rainy season is from early June to mid July. Summer is very hot and humid, though the mountain is a few degrees cooler than the city of Kyoto. Late summer/early fall is typhoon season.

Trees and Plants

The most common trees are Japanese maples, and the evergreen conifers called cryptomeria. There are also pine trees, fragrant olives, mountain cherry, and the occasional bamboo. The most common plants are ferns and mosses. There are also camellia hedges, which bloom all winter. There is a plant that grows up trees, which looks like baby tears, and a number of varieties of the mushroom. There is even Kurama moss (Selaginella remotifolia)

Animals on Kurama

The first floor of Kurama's museum shows the animals that exist in the area, however, few visitors see them, as they tend to stay away from humans. Visitors to the mountain should know about three relatively rare animal hazards, which are posted on the mountain, but only in Japanese. There is a type of poisonous snake and there have been bears reported on the wild half of the mountain. On occasion, wild monkeys have been known to show up on Kurama, and have a great fondness for grabbing cameras, glasses, and food from curious visitors. One unique animal the author was fortunate enough to see is called a tanuki, which is a creature native to Asia, and looks like a cross between a raccoon, a dog and a cat. There are also large snails, small crabs in the water pools, squirrels and birds. In the little Kibune River, the visitor may see a bird called a 'brown dipper.' The dipper looks like a large, brown robin, and it actually walks under the water of the river to forage. The Kurama museum also mentions the presence of flying squirrels and deer.

How High is Kurama Mountain?

Kurama is not a tall mountain, making it an ideal day hike. Kurama is 1870 feet above sea level. The village of Kurama is about half way up the mountain, at an elevation of about 1000 feet. A more practical measure of elevation for hikers is relative to the main gate of the temple. The following elevations are measured from the entryway to Kurama.

Niōmon Entryway- 0 meters
Tahōtō Pagoda- 394 feet (120 meters)
Yuki Shrine- 164 feet (50 meters)
Main Hall- 525 feet (160 meters)

Measuring stone, the highest point on the trail-
771 feet (235 meters)
Inner Temple- 607 feet (185 meters)
Kibune Shrine -115 feet (35 meters)

EMPERORS AND EMPRESSES

Kurama has been loosely connected to the emperor and the
aristocracy since Kyoto became Japan's capital. Only a seven-
mile ride outside that city, Kurama was a pleasant escape from
the hot and humid heat of summer for the Imperial Court.
The name Kurama means saddled Horse Mountain. One

prominent story of how the mountain got its name is that the Emperor gave it to the mountain because of Temmu, who in 683 AD fled from Prince Otomo and left a saddled horse, tied up on this mountain.

The Emperor first recognized Kurama Temple as the capital's northern guardian in the ninth century. A later emperor was fond of Kurama Mountain's vast trees, and insisted that Kurama Mountain be treated as a sanctuary. Fortunately Kurama Mountain has never been logged of its trees, so many of the old trees remain. The Empress Teimei visited Kurama Mountain in 1924. She was also known as Princess Sadako. The Shinden building, near the Amida Buddha Temple, was originally built as a reception hall for her visit. A bench along the path was also built in her honor. The Empress was the wife of the Emperor Taisho. They reigned from 1912- 1926. The Empress was the mother of Emperor Hirohito, who led Japan during WWII. The empress publicly objected to Japan's involvement in WWII, which caused a rift with her son. My Japanese translator related that, "We Japanese believe that Hirohito was forced to start the war because of the fanatic Japanese military."

On Reiki

There are many, many Reiki books and places to go for more information. It is out of the scope of this book to include more than the following.

William Rand - William Rand is the president of the International Center for Reiki Training. He wrote what is still my favorite Reiki book: *Reiki: The Healing Touch*. The center has the world's most extensive basic website on Reiki, www. Reiki.org and publishes the Reiki News magazine, and online newsletter. I liked the center so much, I joined the organization as a teacher in 1995.

Laurelle Shanti Gaia - Director of Teacher Licensing, International Center for Reiki Training. Laurelle is the author of *The Book On Karuna Reiki®*, and *Be Peace Now*. She is the founder of the Infinite Light Healing Studies Center, Inc. in Sedona, AZ, the publishers of this book. Information on the teacher licensing program for the ICRT can be accessed from her website at www.reikiclasses.com

Jessica Miller - Jessica's Reiki website is www.ReikiMastery.com. Her website has articles on Reiki's history, special Reiki techniques, more information about Kurama Mountain and other subjects of interest to Reiki students and teachers.

On Japanese Reiki

The following are people with resources for more information about Japanese Reiki. It is not intended to be an exhaustive list, but is the list of those Jessica has had personal contact with, and found helpful as resources.

Tadao Yamaguchi - : www.jikidenreiki.org Teaches classes in Kyoto and elsewhere. His school is called Jikiden Reiki. He learned Reiki from his mother Chiyoko Yamaguchi and others in his family who had learned Reiki directly from Chujiro Hayashi, and later Hayashi's wife. Tadao continues to research Reiki's roots, and has a number of interesting photos and anecdotes of Reiki's beginnings, some of which are described in *The Hayashi Reiki Manual*. He is also aware of traditional Japanese Healing Techniques, some of which will be included in future books. While most of his classes are in Japanese, he does periodically teach classes for foreigners in English.

Hyakuten Inamoto - www.KomyoReiki.com. A Buddhist priest and Reiki master who speaks excellent English (as well as Japanese), Hyakuten has had the honor of being able to translate and learn from many Japanese Reiki teachers, including

Chiyoko Yamaguchi, and brings to Reiki his own gentle, generous style. He is based in Osaka, and teaches and runs a healing night regularly in Kyoto as well. His school is called KoMyo Reiki. Both English and Japanese speakers are welcome.

Toshitaka Mochizuki is the founder of the Vortex School of Reiki based in Tokyo. It is based on a combination of western and Japanese teachings. He has written several books in Japanese on Reiki, which he hopes to have translated into English. Even the Japanese versions are interesting for non-Japanese to look at. He has done a manga comic book version of the history of Reiki, and the book also contains several photos, including one of the original Usui Reiki Ryoho Gakkai, with Mikao Usui seated in the picture.

Hiroshi Doi- homepage3.nifty.com/GendaiReiki is in English. His Japanese web site is www.gendaireiki.net. I have not trained with Hiroshi Doi, but I have met him on a day Hyakuten was leading him and his students on a tour of Kurama. He calls his school of Reiki Gendai Reiki. While originally trained in western Reiki, he is a member of Reiki Ryoho Gakkai, and has been an excellent source of information on Japanese Reiki Techniques and the Japanese version of Reiki's history. Typically his classes are in Japanese, but he does teach classes periodically with translators.

Frank Arjava Petter - www.Reikidharma.com. He is the author of a number of Japanese Reiki related books, and has been a key researcher into the history of Reiki and Japanese Reiki Techniques. Some of his books include *Reiki: The Legacy of Dr. Usui*, *Reiki Fire*, and he is the co-author of *The Hayashi Healing Manual* with Tadao Yamaguchi.

Rick Rivard - www.threshold.ca/reiki. His ReikiThreshold website is an excellent resource for the evolving information on the history of Reiki. He is an avid researcher and continues to add interesting historical information to his site.

On Kyoto

There are many guides and websites which offer the visitor information on Kyoto and Japan. The following are a couple of less well-known resources you might want to check out.

Judith Clancy's *Exploring Kyoto: On Foot in the Ancient Capital*; (published by Weatherhill 1997) is an excellent guidebook to Kyoto. It is one of the few guides to the area to have more than a paragraph or so about Kurama Mountain.

Kansai Time Out – www.kto.co.jp/ This monthly magazine is full of news, events and ideas for those living in the greater Kyoto area.

Kyoto Journal – www.KyotoJournal.org This is an excellent journal of thought- provoking articles from Asia. Written by volunteers, it provides a variety of perspectives on a wide range of topics.

Kyoto Visitors Guide - www.kyotoguide.com This guide is available at most major hotels in Kyoto and has an excellent website. This is one of the first publications to pick up when coming to Kyoto as it lists all upcoming events (including temple flea markets), has good maps, and has articles and information tailored to the traveler.

On Japanese Buddhism

There are many many places to get information on Buddhism. One of my favorites however is the following website. Website: Japanese Shinto and Buddhist Corner www.onmarkproductions.com/html/buddhism.shtml. This excellent website is full of pictures and information about many aspects of Japanese Buddhism and Shinto. It is authoritative, thorough, and well-indexed.

About the Author

Jessica Miller is a Reiki Historian and a Reiki Master teacher. She is a senior level teacher for the International Center for Reiki Training. Jessica has been teaching Reiki since 1992. Jessica splits her time between California and New England, with periodic trips to Japan and Bali. Information on her upcoming classes, lectures, trips and conferences can be found on her web site www.ReikiMastery.com Her first trip to Japan was in February of 2001. Her second trip was in late September of 2001, when she made her first 21- day pilgrimage to Kurama, in honor of Mikao Usui's original 21 days. Her visit in 2002 and subsequent month-long trips in 2003-2006 culminated in the production of this book. In fall 2006, Jessica made her 100th hike up the mountain, and looks forward to many more visits.

Jessica near the Main Temple
on Kurama Mountain.

Why author this book?

When interviewed about the book, Jessica said: As a stranger visiting the mountain, all I found was intriguing mystery. I could not read the signs. I did not know the culture. I could not speak the language. But I was willing and I was fascinated. I couldn't leave it alone. I made my first pilgrimage, going 22 times up the mountain in one month. It did not matter that I did not speak more than a few words of Japanese, didn't know the culture, or Buddhism or Shinto. I kept returning and I kept asking questions. As I spent more and more time on the mountain, people began to come forward with answers to my questions. The energies of the mountain spoke to me. Almost a year later, I decided to write this book, both to increase my understanding, but also to help others who do not have the luxury of spending a month a year in Japan and having all the right people to ask."

If you enjoyed this book, please visit my web site: www.ReikiMastery.com

The ReikiMastery.com includes information on my Reiki class schedule, healing nights, advanced lectures, seminars and healing sessions. While I teach primarily in California, I do lead trips to (and teach classes) at Kyoto and Mt. Kurama (currently yearly), and teach in other locations when invited by a group. You can also sign up for my free newsletter.

Reiki is a fabulous general purpose tool I think everyone on the planet should learn. It is primarily used for strengthening the ki in the body, and thus improving the body's ability to heal itself. It is excellent on everyday things, like aches, bruises, mood, focus and general energy for the day. It is also very helpful for migraines, joint pain and supporting people through serious illness. As an energy source, Reiki can also be used for space clearing (like Feng Shui), improving the atmosphere of home and business and much more. The uses of Reiki are limited only by the imagination.

My classes tend to be informal. I enjoy answering questions, and teaching students ways to discover their own answers. I also highly recommend the other Reiki teachers licensed by the International Center for Reiki Training, most of whom I know personally, who can be found on the Reiki.org website.

A section of the website is dedicated to Kurama Mountain. This will include: new or updated information about any of the subjects discussed in this book, excerpts from your experiences, and how to contact me. There will also be contact information for local (to Japan) Reiki people, guides and translators.

OTHER PUBLICATIONS & PRODUCTIONS BY INFINITE LIGHT HEALING STUDIES CENTER, INC.

BOOKS

The Book On Karuna Reiki®, by Laurelle Shanti Gaia

Be Peace Now…A Course For Peaceweavers,
by Laurelle Shanti Gaia

Reiki for the Soul… The Eleventh Door, by Mari Hall

Reflections on My Eternal Light, by Jan Manzi

AUDIO PROGRAMS AND CDs:

Infinite Spectrum – Color Healing for Beginners, Sacred Circles Journey CD Manifesting through the Angelic Realms, by Laurelle Shanti Gaia, Divine Temple Journey with Arcangel Raphael

FREE ONLINE COURSES:

www.Be PeaceNow.com

Visit us at www.InfiniteLight.com or www.ReikiClasses.com, www.SpiritualStuff4u.com, email: info@infinitelight.com

ADDITIONAL RESOUCRES

ORGANIZATIONS:

Infinite Light Healing Studies Center & Infinite Light
Publications - www.infinitelight.com
International Center for Reiki Training www.reiki.org
International Association of Reiki Practitioners-www.iarp.org
International Reiki Masters who assisted with this project:
Frank Arjava Petter - www.Reikidharma.com
Hiroshi Doi-homepage3.nifty.com/GendaiReiki
Hyakuten Inamoto - www.KomyoReiki.com
Laurelle Shanti Gaia - www.reikiclasses.com
Michael Arthur Baird - www.ReikiDrumming.com
Mari Hall - International Reiki Association www.wisechoices.com
Tadao Yamaguchi's website www.jikidenreiki.org
Author's website: Jessica Miller www.reikimastery.com

ENDNOTES

[†]-A friend told me "I went there [to Kurama] after my aunt died, and said something or other, and they told me no candles or ceremonies for the dead. Kurama may be the only Buddhist temple in the country without ceremonies for the dead. Marry in Shinto, bury in Buddhism. Many people only associate with a Buddhist temple for ceremonies for the dead."[1] Description of Dakini and Inari www.onmarkproductions.com/html/oinari.shtml

[2] Some translated information on the teacher of Yoshitsune appears here, along with a picture of this temple on Kurama in this article on martial arts. www.shinjin.co.jp/kuki/hyoho/philosophy_e.htm. My translator Ayumi provided the alternate spelling.

[3] The Amida Buddha: www.onmarkproductions.com/html/amida.shtml

[4] Sacred rope or spirit rope description www.onmarkproductions.com/html/shrine-guide-2.shtml#shimenawa

[5] Maoson arriving on earth on this stone reference from Judith Clancy's Exploring Kyoto p139-140. The full book reference appears in the resources section near the end of the book.

[6] The American style naming convention was used for western north pacific hurricanes until 1999. agora.ex.nii.ac.jp/digital-typhoon/help/tc-names.html.en.

[7] The Official Guide-book to Kyoto and the Allied Prefectures, published by Meishinha, by the Kyoto (Japan) City Council, publication date 1895 pg 171-172 google books (pg 162-163 actual text) Available online through Google books at. books.google.com/books?vid=OCLC02600346&id=2 m0j8se1mfgC&pg=RA21-PA171-IA5&vq=kurama&dq=kyoto+kurama +guide

[8] One of many great food websites: www.japan-guide.com/e/e2035

[9] A friend who has lived in Japan for 30 + years says that flush toilets became common in the Kyoto area in the 1970s.

[10] Kyoto City Tourism and Culture Information System. (multi-lingual). raku.city.kyoto.jp/sight_e.phtml

[11] Based on Ayumi's translation of Koji Shinraku. The history of Kurama Mountain, section 1. [Book with sun, moon and earth on the cover]. This Japanese book is available at Kurama Temple. A rough English translation of key passages can be found on my website www.reikimastery.com

[12] Based on Ayumi's translation of Koji Shinraku. The history of Kurama Mountain, section 1. [Book with sun, moon and earth on the cover]. This Japanese book is available at Kurama Temple. A rough English translation of key passages can be found on my website www.reikimastery.com

[13] [14] The translation I have has the name as Karino Hogan Motonobo, however the dates match the lifetime for Kano Motonobu who is one of the most famous artists in Japanese history.

[15] The Official Guide-book to Kyoto and the Allied Prefectures, published by Meishinha, by the Kyoto (Japan) City Council, publication date 1895 pg 171-172 google books (pg 162-163 actual text) Available online through Google books at. books.google.com/books?vid=OCLC026003 46&id=2m0j8se1mfgC&pg=RA21-PA171-IA5&vq=kurama&dq=kyoto +kurama+guide

[16] Another version of the story of Maoson can be found on this martial arts site:
www.shinjin.co.jp/kuki/hyoho/philosophy_e.htm#n7

[17] Sanat Kumara definition from www.esoteric-philosophy.net/glossary.html

[18] based on Ayumi's translation of Subwete Wa Soten Nite Mashimasu (All exist in the respectable heaven) Section 1: Invisible world.

[19] Thanks to Aric Mills for this suggestion.

[20] The version of the Heart Sutra used is from the web site: www.members.aol.com/kyosan1/heart.htm. (With a few minor changes from a Buddhist friend of mine) Another more detailed explanation can be found at: www.andrew-may.com/zendynamics/heart.htm.

[21] Hindu Gods and Goddess in Japan, by Saroj Kumar Chaudhuri, Vedams eBooks (P) Ltd. 2003 ISBN 8179360091. This book covers the stories of Kurama's founding in far more detail than I have used here. (I bought a copy, but you can find it on google books)

[22] Based on Ayumi's rough translation of Subwete Wa Sonten Nite Mashimasu
All exists in Sonten: A summary of the teachings of Mt. Kurama. More of the text available on my website.

[23] Hindu Gods and Goddess in Japan, by Saroj Kumar Chaudhuri, Vedams eBooks (P) Ltd. 2003 ISBN 8179360091 (I bought a copy, but you can find it on google books)

[24] A couple sources which reference the meteor (and include other information)
http://www.shinjin.co.jp/kuki/suigun/konjin_e.htm
http://www.geocities.com/fascin8or/reiki_kuramayama.html

[25] This is from Ayumi's translation of Koji Shinraku. The history of Kurama Mountain, section 1. [Book with sun, moon and earth on the cover]. This Japanese book is available at Kurama temple. A rough English translation of key passages can be found on my website www.reikimastery.com

[26] www.onmarkproductions.com/html/shaka.shtml

[27] www.pref.nara.jp/nara/kaido/eg/ko_nara/spot/k16.htm

[28] Jaanus Japanese Art User and Network System
www.aisf.or.jp/~jaanus/deta/y/yuuzuunenbutsuengi.htm

[29] The Catalpa Bow: A Study of Shamanistic Practices in Japan (Japan Library Classics) by Carmen Blacker, 1975, 1986, 1999 pg 184

[30] www.reikidharma.com/en/reiki/news/en_news14.html

[31] More information on the tengu can be found at:
www.onmarkproductions.com/html/tengu.shtml

[32] Seimei Shrine - www.taleofgenji.org/seimei.html

[33] -(Kippu News Dec 22, 2004
www.kippo.or.jp   /KansaiWindowHtml/News/2004-e/20041222_NEWS.HTML))

[34] pg. 35, Ninja: The Invisible Assasins by Andrew Adams,
ISBN: 089750030X Publisher: Black Belt Communications, 1989

[35] pg. 42, The Lone Samurai: The Life of Miyamoto Musashi by William Scott Wilson, ISBN:477002942X Publisher: Kodansha International
2004

[36] pg 32, Ninja: The Invisible Assasins by Andrew Adams, ISBN: 089750030X Publisher: Black Belt Communications, 1989

[37] pg. 200, The Lone Samurai: The Life of Miyamoto Musashi by William Scott Wilson, ISBN:477002942X Publisher: Kodansha International
2004

[38] pg. 40, The Lone Samurai: The Life of Miyamoto Musashi by William Scott Wilson, ISBN:477002942X Publisher: Kodansha International
2004

[39] [web reference www.shinjin.co.jp/kuki/hyoho/philosophy_e.htm]

[40] [http://uk.geocities.com/bcdojo/kukishinden.htm]

[41] (www.aikidoaus.com.au/dojo/docs/weaphist.htm)

[42] pg 18, Meditation & the Martial Arts by Michael L Raposa ISBN: 0813922380 Publisher: University of Virginia Press, 2003

[43] pg 19, Meditation & the Martial Arts by Michael L Raposa ISBN: 0813922380 Publisher: University of Virginia Press, 2003

[44] [web reference www.shinjin.co.jp/kuki/hyoho/philosophy_e.htm]

[45] For more information: www.sshe.murdoch.edu.au/intersections/issue4/tims_review.html